Pennine Way

Dalesman Publishing Company
Stable Courtyard, Broughton Hall,
Skipton, North Yorkshire BD23 3AE

First Edition 1997

Text © Terry Marsh 1997
Cover: Near Kinder Downfall by John Gillham
Maps by Martin Collins
Printed by Amadeus Press, Huddersfield

A British Library Cataloguing in Publication
record is available for this book

ISBN 185568 108 0

Pennine Way

Terry Marsh

DALESMAN

The Pennine Way

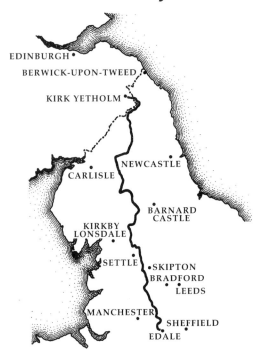

EDINBURGH •

BERWICK-UPON-TWEED •

KIRK YETHOLM •

NEWCASTLE

CARLISLE

BARNARD
CASTLE

KIRKBY
LONSDALE

SETTLE

SKIPTON
BRADFORD
LEEDS

MANCHESTER

SHEFFIELD
EDALE

Contents

Introduction

Inspired by correspondence with two American girls who wrote to him asking for advice about a tramping holiday in England, journalist and outdoor campaigner Tom Stephenson went on to write in the Daily Herald of 22 June 1935 "...why should we not press for something akin to the Appalachian Trail – a Pennine Way from the Peak to the Cheviots?"

"This need be no Euclidean line, but a meandering way deviating as needs be to include the best of that long range of moor and fell; no concrete or asphalt track, but just a faint line on the Ordnance Maps which the feet of grateful pilgrims would, with the passing years, engrave on the face of the land."

Tom Stephenson's proposal gained much support from among the fast-growing outdoor movement, but with numerous new rights of way needing to be created it was 30 years before the route opened in 1965 as Britain's first long distance footpath.

The original idea was to stick as much as possible to the crest of the Pennines, linking old footpaths, drove roads, packhorse routes, bridleways, shepherds' and miners' tracks, and even Roman roads. Modifications were necessary here and there, and the odd idiosyncratic lurch, as from Teesdale to Dufton, introduced to include places of scenic interest or to reach a valley where food and lodging could be found. But the end product was a superb undertaking in almost any sense of the word, one that began a long- and middle-distance footpath revolution, so much so that the whole country now seems to be covered in them.

Conceived and generally followed in a south to north direction, the Pennine Way begins in Edale, a popular base for the active Manchester and Sheffield ramblers of the 1930s, and indeed today. The route tackles first the vastness of the Kinder and Bleaklow massifs, treading a course to the northern edge of the Peak National Park at Standedge. There it passes into the noticeably different landscapes of the South Pennines, crossing the Calder valley and heading for the famed land of the Brontës.

Beyond lies the unrivalled limestone beauty of the Yorkshire Dales National Park, which the Way enters near Gargrave on the River Aire, and leaves at the highest pub in England, the Tan Hill. In between, the extravagant scenery for which the Dales are renowned excites a host of impressions in sensitive walkers, and contrasts markedly with the austere landscapes of the South Pennines and Peak.

A return to wild countryside lies beyond the Tan Hill Inn as the route heads into the North Pennines, an area that has borne more than its share of mining activity, and still carries the scars to prove it. Here many consider the Pennine Way is at its best as it courts the turbulent, boisterous Tees, tackles the long crossing of the Pennines to visit High Cup Nick and the remote village of Dufton, before getting to grips with Cross Fell and its acolytes, the three highest summits in the Pennines. Beyond Cross Fell, the Way eases down to the village of Garrigill and on beside the North Tyne to the cobbled streets of Alston, a long-established market town. It then heads along the ancient Maiden Way, a Roman supply road, to reach that outstanding glory of the far-flung Roman Empire, Hadrian's Wall.

Another distinct change of scenery occurs beyond the Wall, as the route heads for the Border forests and the delectable Cheviot Hills, a region that in times gone by has witnessed inordinate savagery, bloodshed and turmoil during a period known as the Border Troubles, a complex and vividly interesting period of British history recounted by George MacDonald Fraser in his book *The Steel Bonnets*.

Finally, clinging to every last inch and centimetre of high ground, the Way enters the rolling hills of southern Scotland, a delightful prospect, but which by no stretch of imagination can be thought of as the Pennines. The route enters its last lap to slip gracefully down to an end at Kirk Yetholm, where the Border Hotel has acquired a certain notoriety in the annals of Pennine Way history for welcoming weary wanderers.

The Pennine Way Co-ordination Project

The Pennine Way passes through numerous local authorities, all of which have an input to the management of the route. The Pennine Way Co-ordination Project, however, set up by the Countryside Commission, and based in Mytholm-royd, Calderdale, was established in 1989 to undertake the first full condition survey of the Pennine Way. Since that time the project has been closely involved with the gathering of user information and other research. It also works in partnership with the managing authorities to complete restoration, and undertakes development work into new path management techniques.

In practical terms for the walker this means that large stretches of the Pennine Way have had to be improved because of the erosion caused by its own popularity and the harshness of the conditions that exist throughout its length. In 1989, before the main restoration programme commenced, the areas of significant path damage were mainly on the deep blanket peat moorlands. These included all the moors in the Peak National Park, namely the Kinder, Bleaklow, Black Hill and the Saddleworth Moors; Blackstone Edge to Standedge; sections between the Walshaw reservoirs and Top Withins; Ickornshaw Moor; Great Shunner Fell; sections of the Cumbrian Fells between Cow Green in Teesdale and Cross Fell; and the Border Ridge and The Cheviot. Work on these sections is still on-going in places, and walkers can expect to find significantly improved walking conditions where previously bog-floundering was the order of the day.

Anyone wanting more information about the work of the Project or about the Pennine Way should contact the Pennine Way Co-ordination Project, Clegg Nook, Cragg Road, Mytholmroyd, West Yorkshire, HX7 5EB, which produces an excellent information sheet called "The Pennine Way: Information for Students and Researchers, or All you ever wanted to know about the Pennine Way (but were afraid to ask)".

Planning the walk

It would be foolhardy to think that you could simply turn up at Edale (or Kirk Yetholm) and just set off. Even if you are planning to do the walk in short stages, some forethought must be given to the logistics of what is involved.

In 1989 the Pennine Way was 314 miles (502km) in total, including loops. By 1994, rationalisation of some of the misalignments had reduced this to 289 miles (463km); the recommended route is today 268 miles (429km), though the section distances given in the main text add up to a lesser figure. This is because it is extremely difficult to measure such a long route in exactly the same way and with it the same precision as those whose job it is to work closely with the route on a day-to-day basis.

Most walkers intending to go the whole way should allow at least two full weeks for the walk, though more days should be allowed if possible to introduce rest days, which can be vital for everyone but the strongest and most experienced long-distance walkers.

Inevitably, there are long days and short days, with the two most demanding coming at either end, whichever direction is taken. Edale to Crowden involves tackling the Kinder and Bleaklow massifs, with only the Snake Pass road as a point at which outside assistance, or a lift, can be obtained. At the other end, the final stretch from Byrness to Kirk Yetholm has only two emergency shelters or a long detour to isolated farmsteads providing accommodation. For a suggested itinerary, see the section "How to use this guide" on page 20. In spite of this, no attempt has been made to configure the guide into daily sections, though it may seem that way. The book is constructed in five sections, but these are of geographical and editorial significance only. To break the route up into sections of lesser length, so that each ended at a place where accommodation might be found, would make the book impractical. Of greater importance is the need for walkers to decide their own daily dose, and to plan accordingly, regardless of the structure of this guidebook.

Finally, the Countryside Commission produce several useful leaflets, including the Pennine Way Update (covering details of realignments), and Pennine Way CCP366 (a general information leaflet). These are usually available free from tourist information and visitor centres or by post from the Countryside Commission Postal Sales, PO Box 124, Walgrave, Northampton, NN6 9TL.

Accommodation

Only walkers with previous backpacking experience should consider undertaking the Pennine Way in this manner. It is simply too arduous and demanding an exercise on which to cut one's teeth in backpacking, and the requirements of such an approach call for detailed planning based on experience. Otherwise, more conventional accommodation should be used. This ranges from youth hostels and bunkhouses to B&Bs, guest houses and hotels. There are, however, long sections in the north and south where there is only limited availability of accommodation, making it essential that walkers plan their overnight stops well in advance. A most comprehensive guide to accommodation is available from John Needham of The Pennine Way Association, 23 Woodland Crescent, Hilton Park, Prestwich, Manchester, M25 8WQ. Send a stamped addressed envelope and £1 to cover costs (or a higher sum if you feel you might like to contribute to the work of the association). Alternatively you could become a member of the association.

Public transport

While it might seem reasonable to assume that anyone venturing out into the countryside is aware of fundamental environmental issues like pollution and congestion, there still appears to be an assumption that everyone who does so travels by car. It is certainly true that it is becoming increasingly difficult to travel anywhere on foot that is totally free from the sound of traffic of one sort or another.

Pennine Wayfarers are in a position to do something about it, if only in a very small way, by making use of public transport to facilitate their walking. Those tackling the whole route in one go will find that unless someone runs them to the start and picks them up from the end, they have no choice in the matter. But even where they can arrange lifts, it would be a gesture towards the countryside through which they have just walked or intend to walk to approach it by environmentally friendly means.

Walkers intending to do the Pennine Way in stages are in a better position to make greater use of public transport. All that is needed is a current rail or bus timetable and a little bit of pre-planning. Up-to-date information about public transport is included in the accommodation guide provided by the Pennine Way Association, but the following will give some indication of the possibilities, or you can call the nearest tourist information office.

Edale: By trains to and from Manchester (Piccadilly) and Sheffield, and Snake summit. 0345 484950

Crowden: Buses between Manchester and Sheffield. 0990 808080

Marsden: Via trains from Manchester to Huddersfield and Leeds.

Stanedge: Buses between Huddersfield and Oldham run to Manchester on Saturdays.

Hebden Bridge: Trains from Liverpool, Manchester, Preston, Todmorden and Leeds, including Sunday service. 0345 484950

Haworth: Private Worth Valley rail line stops at Haworth, connection to main line at Keighley.

Cowling: Bus service.

Thornton-in-Craven: Buses between Colne, Earby and Skipton. Trains from Colne and Skipton connecting with Leeds and Manchester. 01756 749215

Gargrave: Bus and train service, connecting to Skipton, Settle and Malham. 01756 749215

Malham: Bus service to Skipton via Gargrave. 01756 749215

Horton-in-Ribblesdale: Bus and rail service via Settle.

Hawes: Bus service to Richmond, connecting to Darlington. Bus service links with Hawes and the Settle-Carlisle line. 01325 468771

Thwaite and Keld: Bus service to Richmond. 01325 468771

Bowes: Bus service to Barnard Castle, connecting to Darlington.

Middleton-in-Teesdale: Bus service to Darlington. 01325 468771

Dufton: No direct link, but a rail service to Appleby on Leeds-Settle-Carlisle line.

Alston: Bus service from Alston to Haltwhistle via Slaggyford, and from Alston to Penrith. 01434 381200

Greenhead: Bus service. 01946 63222

Bellingham: Coach service to Hexham, connecting to rail service at Newcastle. 01434 602217

Byrness: Bus services from Bellingham, and from Newcastle and Edinburgh. 0990 808080

Kirk Yetholm: Bus service to Kelso, connecting to Jedburgh, Newcastle and Edinburgh. 01573 224141

Walking conditions

It has been argued that the construction of causeways across the most badly-eroded sections of the Way has improved the overall walking conditions. But this is a false assumption. Certainly, the days of floundering through vast boggy expanses are gone, but nothing else has changed, and the route is still extremely demanding throughout its length. Many consider that the flagstones that have been used have created a hard surface where none existed, and that this will take its toll on weary legs.

The major restoration work commenced in 1990, at a time when there was still heavy dependence on boardwalks and imported aggregates and geotextile rafts. Latterly two methods of path construction have been used.

One is known as soil reorganisation and Hymacing, which had been trialled north of the Border on the West Highland Way and the Southern Upland Way. This involves digging mineral subsoils from beneath the blanket peat and depositing these on the surface to make a mineral-based walking surface of local materials.

The second method, originated on the Pennine Way but also used on the West Pennine Moors, has been to use the traditional flag or causey pathways. These causeways were a prominent feature of the 17th- and 18th-century landscape, and evolved to serve the packhorse trains. This method involves the use of recycled materials, mainly Rossendale mill flagstones, often involving the wholesale acquisition of old mill floors. Rossendale stone offers a rough surface and a good range of natural colours.

Because this work is still on-going, no attempt, other than a nominal one, has been made in the text to identify those sections which have already been treated and those on which work is continuing. To do so renders this guidebook out-of-date before it is published. Walkers may therefore feel able to express considerable delight if a particular notorious stretch of bogland is found to be flagged, or navigation across a bleak section of moorland suddenly becomes easier as a result of flagging.

Weather

The best weather in the Pennines is usually recorded from mid-May to September, with June normally being the best month – though June of 1993, when blizzard conditions prevailed, was an exception. Even so, the high Pennines in particular suffer heavy rainfall and are invariably windswept. Summer weather patterns in Britain seem to be changing all the time, and may include everything from low cloud and mist, to burning sun. Walkers should be prepared for any kind of weather.

Equipment, safety and supplies

All walkers have their own preferences for equipment and clothing, but the following may be a useful reminder – rucksack (comfortable and padded), boots, socks (and spares), trousers (or shorts, etc.), underclothes, shirt, midwear (e.g. pullover) and spare, wind- and waterproof jacket and overtrousers, hat, gloves, maps, compass, torch (with spare battery and bulb), whistle, first aid kit, survival bag or space blanket, food and drink as necessary, insect repellent, ablution tackle, including half a roll of toilet tissue for emergencies, and a small hand towel.

Backpackers will also need such weighty items as a tent, sleeping bag, Karrimat (or equivalent), cooking equipment and utensils. It is useful, too, to carry a few pedal bin liners, which can serve many purposes, notably separating wet and dry clothing, carrying rubbish, containing burst packs of food, and for insulating dry socks from wet boots when walking.

Remember to allow for a marked lack of "hole-in-the-wall" cash dispensers, and be sure you are carrying enough cash, plus a cheque book and banker's card. Not everyone accepts credit cards.

It is vital that everyone undertaking the Pennine Way knows basic safety in mountains. Many parts are close to outside help, but equally many parts are very distant from assistance, where the walker is on his or her own and needs to be self-sufficient. There are numerous books on the subject of safety on the hills, but if you are at the stage where you need to be told what they are, then realistically you are not ready to tackle the Pennine Way.

There are quite a few stretches of the Way where the opportunity does not exist to stock up on supplies, plus many where the chance exists, but poor timing, a late start, or delays caused by bad weather, may mean that you arrive after the shops have closed. All these considerations must be taken into account, but remember that it is unwise to move into a long and exposed section of route with depleted supplies that you have not had the opportunity to replenish. A better decision would be to wait until the following day to move on.

Waymarking

The Pennine Way is for the most part adequately and sensitively waymarked, though there are long stretches of open moorland where the ability to navigate closely and correctly is of paramount importance. Because the route is so well signposted and waymarked, the text of this guide does not insult the intelligence of the reader by giving a detailed route description where none is needed, leaving the walker free to take in the surroundings without having to resort to a complex set of instructions. Where detail is needed, it will be found.

In addition to diversions to combat erosion, there are many other places where the route is less than ideal. In some places shortcuts have become established, in others walkers have preferred a longer route to a shortcut that is now no longer visible. Some are waymarked, others are not, all of which is confusing. Action is being taken by the authorities to define a clear route, properly waymarked. Because this will take some time, walkers should be aware of the possibility of changes to the route given in this guide.

Maps

The maps accompanying this guide though admirably drawn are purely diagrammatic, and are insufficient for detailed navigation across inhospitable terrain. Wayfarers must carry the relevant Ordnance Survey map, a compass and the knowledge of how to navigate competently.

There are two scales of map available, either the 1:50,000 maps of the OS Landranger series, or the 1:25,000 scale of the Outdoor Leisure Map series. At the time of writing, the OLMs are incomplete between Alston and Byrness, but it is understood that two new OLMs will be introduced in spring 1997 (when this book will be published) which will fill the gap. The relevant maps are:

Landranger

74 Kelso and surrounding area
80 Cheviot Hills and Kielder Forest area
86 Haltwhistle, Bewcastle and Alston area
91 Appleby-in-Westmorland
92 Barnard Castle and surrounding area
98 Wensleydale and Upper Wharfedale
103 Blackburn, Burnley and surrounding area
109 Manchester and surrounding area
110 Sheffield and Huddersfield area

Outdoor Leisure

1 The Peak District: The Dark Peak
2 Yorkshire Dales: Western area
10 Yorkshire Dales: Southern area
16 The Cheviot Hills
21 South Pennines
30 Yorkshire Dales: Northern and Central areas
31 North Pennines: Teesdale and Weardale
42 Kielder Water
43 Hadrian's Wall

In addition, Harveys maps have produced a number of maps that cover some of the Way, e.g. the Peak. In the near future, they may also produce a strip map for the Pennine Way.

How to use this guide

The guide is essentially in three parts: this section contains all the support information, another contains the route descriptions in a south to north configura-tion; the third gives a route description from north to south. The main route description also gives background information of a local, social and historical nature, separated from the main route description so that the route can be followed without having to wade through the supporting infor-mation. To avoid needless repetition the north to south description does not contain this background infor-mation, though it does mean that the walker travelling in that direction will have to cross-reference to the main text for information about things met up with along the way.

The route description is given in bite sized chunks, although these are not intended to be recommended daily dosages. With the aid of the accommodation guide (from the Pennine Way Association), everyone should be able to plan their own itineraries. If you do follow the sections given in this guide, they add up as shown in the table opposite. The discrepancy between the above approximate figures, and the official distances is not significant. The end result is that the Pennine Way represents a walk of around 250 miles (400km), and at least 18 days of walking.

Quite what Tom Stephenson would think of his brainchild now is anyone's guess. Its success has grown out of all proportion. The lowest estimates of annual use are that there are 8-12,000 long distance walkers and 220-240,000 day walkers on the whole route. Whether the feet of the "pilgrims" are indeed grateful is debatable, and, time has shown, "engraved" should now read "scoured". But, on balance, it would be comforting to think that he was happy with his idea, and everything that has since flowed from it.

Section	Miles	Km
1: The Dark Peak		
Edale to Crowden	16	25.5
Crowden to Standedge	11¼	18
2: The South Pennines		
Standedge to Hebden Bridge	15	24
Hebden Bridge to Ponden	11	17.5
Ponden to Cowling/Ickornshaw	3½	6
3: The Yorkshire Dales		
Cowling to Thornton-in-Craven	6	10
Thornton-in-Craven to Malham	10½	17
Malham to Horton-in-Ribblesdale	14	22.5
Horton-in-Ribblesdale to Hawes	14	22.5
Hawes to Keld	12	20
Keld to Tan Hill	3½	6
4: The North Pennines		
Tan Hill to Middleton	16	25.5
As above but via Bowes Loop	20	32
Middleton to Dufton	17	28
Dufton to Alston	19	30
Alston to Greenhead	16	26
5: The Cheviot Hills		
Greenhead to Bellingham	21	33.5
Bellingham to Byrness	14	23
Byrness to Kirk Yetholm	25	40
As above plus The Cheviot	27	44
Totals	244¾	395

1   The Dark Peak

Beginning its journey in the village of Edale, the Pennine Way visits the northern part of the Peak National Park, the first of ten national parks established between 1951 and 1957. Surrounded on all sides by the industrial conurbations described by William Blake as a Golgotha of "dark, Satanic mills", the Peak possesses many unique qualities, not least that of providing a vast oasis of freedom from the grimness of the neighbouring large manufacturing towns and cities of the north.

The northern part of the Peak is known as the Dark Peak. The old name of the region is Peakland, appearing in the Anglo-Saxon Chronicle of 924AD as Peaclond, meaning the land of the hill dwellers rather than the land of the peaks. In Saxon times, the Peak lay on the northern edge of the Kingdom of Mercia, and its people were called Pecsaetna – Pec from the Old English peac, meaning a hill, and saetna from saete or saetan, meaning dwellers.

So, the first stage of the northbound Pennine Way traverses the Dark Peak, a region hugely different, in many ways, from the limestone landscapes to the south, for here the landscape is a vast expanse of wild, gritstone moorland, topped with heather, bilberry and hardy, resilient grasses. The region's attempts at fame, however, often flounder among the numerous peaty groughs (steep-sided water courses cut into the peat, often down to the bare bones of underlying rock) that bedevil almost every part of the landscape.

Daniel Defoe, who travelled through the Peak and northwards into the South Pennines in the 18th century, positively hated the area, describing it as "the most desolate, wild and abandoned country in all England", though his view of things may have been coloured by its reputation in court circles as a place of exile for recalcitrant wives.

Pennine Wayfarers need first to tackle the great plateau of Kinder (pronounced Kin-der, rather than Kind-er), though the attentions of far too many walkers have resulted in a change to the original line of the Pennine Way to the former bad weather alternative route – which is distinctly kinder. Even so, until recent times the northern part of the Kinder plateau, known as Featherbed Moss, had a vile reputation among walkers as a sliddery, shifting, slimy, slutchy swamp that simply could not be avoided. Path renovation work has tamed this beast, quite for how long remains to be seen.

North of Kinder, those who delight in peaty, gritty moorlands will be delighted to learn that yet more await, in the form of Bleaklow. Again, most of the worst sections of the Pennine Way have been improved by renovation work that raises the vexed question of whether the "wilderness exploration" of Britain's long distance trails should be managed, or left to be addressed by each visitor's own cunning and determination. Will it become a hard-surfaced motorway? Will it then still be the Pennine Way?

Beyond Bleaklow, the Way presses on over Black Hill, again a notorious stretch, across which the worst stretches have been subdued, before finally reaching the northern extremity of the Peak National Park at Standedge Cutting, and the A62.

Edale to Crowden

16 miles (25.5km)

Daily Telegraph contributor J H B Peel once said of Edale that it "has had thrust upon itself the greatness of being both an alpha and an omega of Britain's longest footpath". In spite of this accolade, Edale goes about its daily life in an unruffled way, accommodating the rucksack-laden hopefuls setting off northwards to Kirk Yetholm, and receiving, no doubt laden with a mixture of delight and sadness, those who have travelled in the opposite direction.

Yet Edale is more than the small, equable village occupying a position at the western end of the Hope valley. The broad green valley itself is "most people's gateway to the Dark Peak", as Roly Smith, Head of Information to the Peak National Park, describes it in his book First and Last. *Perhaps Edale is best described as a gateway, something you pass through on your way to somewhere else, for so it is, as Peel comments, "nothing has ever happened at Edale; no battle, no ducal elopement, not even a local lad who manufactured a knighthood". You come to Edale with the express intention of leaving it, which is exactly what the northbound Pennine Way does.*

Unfortunately in so doing, the Pennine Way has created an erosion problem of monumental proportions, facing wayfarers with a dilemma even before setting off. Do we use the original line, still a right of way, or accept the necessity of making amendments to routes as problems arise? To do the latter is to act responsibly and to ease the pressure on the eroded plateau moorlands of Kinder. More fundamentally, to follow what used to be described as the bad weather alternative is considerably easier, scarcely any further, and a far more certain way of getting you to Kinder Downfall, your first major objective, than navigating through the homogeneous peat channels above Grindsbrook Clough, which are very confusing in poor visibility. For these reasons, the revised Pennine Way should be followed, a deviation from the original, but a necessary action that will be encountered again as you head north. Since the Pennine Way begins at the Old Nag's Head in Edale, visits the highest pub in the country, and finishes at the Border Hotel in Kirk Yetholm, it could be argued that the Pennine Way is no more than the ultimate pub walk. If you can take comfort from such knowledge your first steps, from the Old Nag's Head, will be taken in joyous anticipation.

By a path just opposite the Old Nag's Head take a well-worn path west for Upper Booth and Hayfield by farm and barn, hedgerows of hawthorn and holly, rowan and birch, and over a stile to cross the southern slopes of Broadlee Bank Tor.

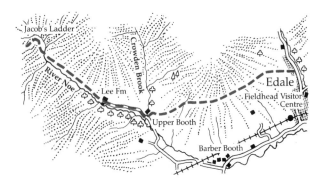

The rim of the slopes that rise greenly on the right forms part of a popular walk known as Kinder Southern Edges, studded with weather-worn outcrops of rock that have acquired names such as Crowden Tower, Wool Packs, Pym Chair and Noe Stool. To the south the view is across the River Noe to the swelling flanks of Rushup Edge and Mam Tor, a fine ridge regarded as the dividing line between the White and Dark Peaks.

Signposted where it needs to be, the Way presses on over a grassy rise and down to meet a track that leads to Upper Booth Farm and a surfaced lane beyond. Turn right soon to cross Crowden Brook, and then through a gate to Lee Farm. The unenclosed moorland that lies ahead was crossed by an ancient packhorse trail along which salt would have been conveyed from mines in Cheshire, bringing wool from the sheep farms of Derbyshire and Yorkshire on the return journey. A packhorse bridge, known as Youngate, not far from Lee Farm, bears testimony to this.

Over the bridge the Way tackles a restored zigzag track known as Jacob's Ladder, which slashes casually across the hillside, probing its defences for the easiest line.

The Ladder, described by Ethel Carleton Williams (in her Companion into Derbyshire – 1948), *as "a formidable obstacle in wet weather [on which walkers] have been known to sprain their ankles on the slippery surface", is named after Jacob Marshall, one of the men known as 'jaggers' who drove the packhorse trains. Jacob is reputed to have been in the habit of sending his ponies by the zigzag route while he raced up a shortcut to give himself*

time to smoke a pipe at the top before his ponies arrived.
The scenery is superb, and it gets better as the route rises
higher; great wedges of moorland, purpled in autumn by
heather, stretch as far as the eye can see, an occasional
mountain hare (a species re-introduced more than a
hundred years ago) may appear briefly to add a note of
interest, while the wind bears the call of grouse, curlew,
plover and skylark, drawing walkers ever further into the
wild embrace of Kinder.

The final escape from this western finger of Edale
continues still quite steeply until it reaches a cairn
and a gate below the prominent hump known as
the Swine's Back. The Way branches right here
bound for Edale Rocks, but it is worth walking
ahead for a short distance further to see Edale Cross.

Edale Cross, an isolated boundary marker for the Royal
Forest of the Peak, now enclosed by walls, was also known
as the Champion Cross, a corruption of Champayne, the
name of the southern part of the Forest. Near the point
where the cross stands the three forest wards of Longden-
dale, Ashop and Edale, and Champayne met, and it
would have served both as boundary marker and guide
stone. It is also claimed to have been erected by the Abbot
of Basingwerk Abbey to mark the boundary of the land,
granted to the monks in 1157, though this claim finds
little favour these days. For many years the Cross lay
broken, until, in 1810, it was re-erected by John Gee, a
local farmer, who added the date and his initials.

From the Cross, turn northwards beside a wall,
then trend north-east to rejoin the main route at a
wall gap. Keep going north for a short distance
beside the wall and head uphill to three large

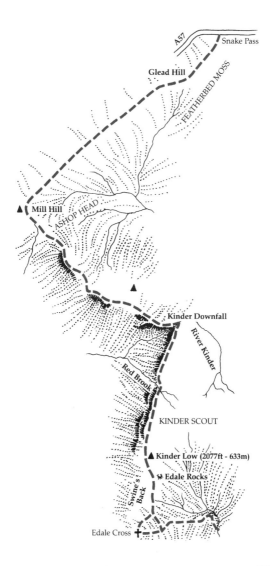

cairns, taking care not to wander off along the prominent path that leads around the Kinder Southern Edges. Before long the path leads to a gritstone outcrop known as Edale Rocks, beyond which the land on the left descends more noticeably and with increasing definition. Keep to the left of the trig pillar on Kinder Low to pursue an occasionally-cairned path leading over rather firmer terrain to the celebrated Kinder Downfall.

In the view westwards the eye is immediately taken by the glint, often grey, of Kinder Reservoir, enfolded by heather-clad hillsides. Beyond, it fades into the industrial murk of Greater Manchester, which only serves to enliven the stride, in search of better landscapes to admire ahead.

To the east squats the blackness of the Kinder Plateau, the sort of place, rather like a scruffy urchin, that only a mother could love. It was once described, by Mrs Humphry Ward in The History of David Grieve, *as "a vast black glacier, whereof the crevasses are great fissures, ebon black in colour, sometimes ten feet deep". The comparison is well earned; Roly Smith's view is not far removed: "The chocolate-brown peat steams, like manure, in the sunshine after rain and spreads in waves like a fossilised ocean to the distant horizon."*

Kinder Downfall is rarely a dramatic sight, but when the River Kinder does manage a force of water it can be awe-inspiring as it plunges over the lip it has fashioned for itself across countless years. In winter it is frequently frozen into a solid display of glittering icicles, but if the wind howls across from Kinder Reservoir there is a good chance waterproofs will be needed, for the puny waters of the river are often thrown back into the air, arcing high above the falls as if considered unfit to grace the valley below. It is a truly spectacular sight.

Beyond Kinder Downfall, the Pennine Way takes a roughly north-westerly course, flirting constantly with dark gritty outcrops and never far from the steep slopes sweeping down to Kinder Reservoir. The path passes through a wall and continues to a large cairn above a steep descent to a rather boggy col at the head of William Clough. Across the col the path presses on, passing not far from a prehistoric flint factory, where flints were fashioned for arrows in the distant past. Before long climb steeply to the top of Mill Hill, from where the route clearly heads north-east, along a broad peaty ridge dotted with the tell-tale heads of cotton grass, a plant that grows only in wet places.

The Way is now bound for the summit of the Snake Road, trending rather more easterly on the approach to Glead Hill, before returning to a north-easterly route as it continues towards Featherbed Moss. On a clear day the Snake Road (A57 Glossop-Sheffield) will now be in view, reached across another expanse of cotton grass, described by Tony Hopkins as "beautiful, soft and white, idly tossed over a sodden black mattress".

The sodden black mattress, however, used to have a notorious reputation as one of the worst sections of the walk, comprising slimy peat groughs. Now all that has been tamed by large paving blocks of stone, which you will encounter on many a section of the Way as you progress northwards. The top of Snake Road, one of Telford's turnpikes constructed in 1821, is predictably known as the Snake Pass, and takes its name from the Snake Inn downhill to the east, rather than the other way round. The inn in turn derives its title from the serpent which is the crest of the Cavendish family, Dukes of Devonshire, who owned great tracts of land around Bleaklow until the estate was taken by the state in lieu of death duties.

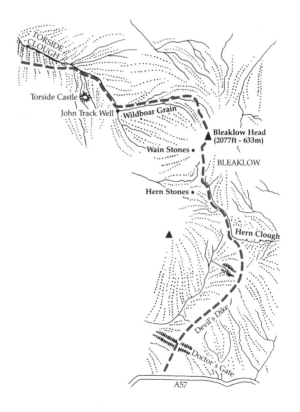

Across the Snake Road, the surfaced Way continues more or less level to reach a crosspath known as Doctor's Gate.

Doctor's Gate is an ancient thoroughfare possibly of Roman origin, linking the forts of Melandra, west of Glossop, with Navio, at Brough, near Castleton. It is thought to be named after Dr. John Talbot, vicar of Glossop between 1494 and 1550, who used the route frequently during the 16th century, though little more is known about him. In the 17th century, the road was known as "Doctor Talbotes Gate", while Camden referred to it as Doctor's Gate in 1789. There is also a tradition that Doctor's Gate links Doctor Faustus and the Devil, or that it is a corruption of Dog Tor, in reference to the profile of nearby gritstone boulders, though there are none now that obviously resemble dogs.

Modern historians, however, are disposed to the view that Doctor's Gate is simply a medieval packhorse route linking two remote valleys.

Beyond Doctor's Gate, the Way leads to Devil's Dyke, a deep furrow through more peat hags the history of which is obscure, though it may be an ancient boundary. The Way continues in the same north-easterly direction to reach Alport Low, just south of Hern Clough, where the route changes direction again, now heading directly for Bleaklow Head via a series of interconnecting groughs.

Here the route is just a short distance from the summit of Bleaklow, set amid a great black swelling of upland that in poor weather can blight any ambition to master this most difficult terrain. Before reaching the top of Bleaklow, and just off the line of the Way, are the Wain Stones, two among many gritstone tors. They have the distinction of appearing to kiss one another, especially when viewed from the south. The highest point of Bleaklow lies just a little way north-north-east of the Wain Stones, a moment of considerable relief since all is now downhill to Crowden.

The summit of Bleaklow, in contrast to its surroundings, is a plateau of sandy gravel with the ever-present peat hags circling it like wolves at bay.

A line of cairns shows the way off Bleaklow, and along paths west to a heathery section above Wildboar Grain, with the views of Longdendale improving all the time. A short way on Wildboar Grain meets Torside Clough, where a diligent search will locate a tiny walled spring, constructed long ago for the benefit of packhorses. This is John Track Well, a source of clean fresh water.

Across Wildboar Grain turn north-west once more, following the upper section of steep-sided Torside Clough. A good path runs delightfully along above the clough as heather becomes more abundant and rock outcrops and boulders start to lend more definition to the landscape. Suddenly Torside Reservoir is in view and the drama of the plateau on Bleaklow soon forgotten.

The final descent to Longdendale is on steep grassy slopes to Reaps Farm then to an old level crossing, now part of the Longdendale Trail for walkers and cyclists. Beyond go down easily to reach the dam of

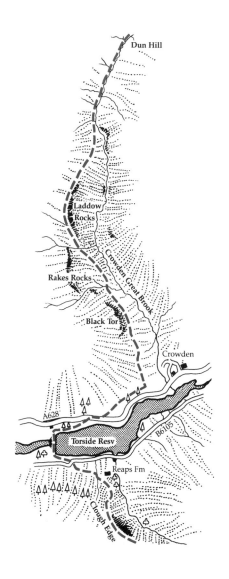

Dun Hill

Laddow
Rocks

Crowden Great Brook

Rakes Rocks

Black Tor

Crowden

A628

Torside Resv

B6105

Reaps Fm

Clough Edge

Torside Reservoir. Across the dam, turn right up a flight of stone steps to a white stile. Here, turn right and ascend through a plantation of pines before rising to meet the A628.

Go half right, east and north-east up a stony trackway, continuing past another plantation to a signpost at which the Pennine Way goes left (northwards), bound for Laddow Rocks. Walkers heading for Crowden, its campsite and/or youth hostel should ignore this left turn, and keep ahead, descending to cross Crowden Brook.

Longdendale is the upper valley of the River Etherow, though you see precious little of the Etherow. Most of its course has succumbed to a succession of large reservoirs – Bottoms, Valehouse, Woodhead, Torside and Rhodeswood – constructed between 1848 and 1862 to serve Manchester and the surrounding towns. Sadly, the reservoirs have never done much to enhance the scenery, and are all too noticeably man-made. To make matters worse, you need only pause above the valley for a while to realise that once it would have been beautiful. Now it is despoiled by roads, telegraph poles, electricity pylons and a disused railway that disappears into the maw of Woodhead Tunnel a few miles to the east.

Crowden to Standedge

11¼ miles (18km)

Although sections of the Way across Black Hill and on to Wessenden Head Moor have seen footpath 'improvements', there is still a goodly measure of the quagmirish nightmare of old awaiting anyone who strays from the path. John Gillham, in Pennine Ways, *describes the trek over Black Hill as "the least interesting section of the entire route [where] the yardsticks of progress are not the mountain-tops but the trans-Pennine roads which parcel the featureless badlands into small sections". It is on this section that the Pennine Way reaches the northern border of the Peak National Park.*

Return from Crowden to the signpost, now turning right to head roughly northwards on a stony track above Crowden Brook, towards Laddow Rocks. For a while the Way stays below the escarpment edge of Black Tor and Rakes Rocks, but then, once beyond Oakenclough Brook which provides a few delightful cascades, it ascends to the top of Laddow Rocks. The rocks, a popular venue for Manchester climbers, are a good place for a brief halt to survey for the last time Bleaklow massif and Wildboar Clough, which is soon to disappear.

The route continues across the top of Laddow Rocks, never far from the edge, and offers a few interesting images of shapely rocks below. Take care not to stray along a path that heads for Chew Reservoir across Laddow Moss.

Chew Reservoir, built in 1912, is regarded by some writers as the highest reservoir in the country, a claim that Cow Green much further north in Teesdale contests. Both reservoirs are almost completely surrounded by the 490m contour, so perhaps a tie is the best result.

The Way continues northwards from Laddow Rocks, generally without difficulty until, beyond Red Ratcher, what was once a morass is now a morass with flagstones across it, making the approach to Black Hill, the top of which bears a trig pillar, considerably less arduous than it was previously.

It wasn't always so easy: Peel wrote, "I doubt that even the sunniest day could relieve the oppressiveness of Black Hill" – but, to be fair, he had just sunk to his knees in the bogs along the top of the hill, so perhaps such a jaundiced view can be forgiven.

Beyond Black Hill, the Way now follows what used to be the alternative route to the A635 at Wessenden Head. It heads north-east from Black Hill's summit to Black Dike Head, just north of Issue Clough, beyond which a rolling landscape leads the eye to the distant town of Holmfirth. The village is renowned as the setting for the television series *Last of the Summer Wine*, and it is easy to see why the producers opted for such an attractive location. With Black Hill behind you, the view is already acquiring the familiar green hue of the summer scenes that were filmed here.

From Black Dike Head the path moves away from Issue Clough to reach a boundary ditch that now leads unerringly down to the road, where the Isle of Skye Inn, demolished in the 1950s, once stood.

"Lonely, isolated" is how Frank Singleton, *in* Lancashire and the Pennines, *described the Isle of Skye Inn, the first of several such remote travellers' inns encountered along the Pennine Way. Don't rely on it, but these days the site of the inn is often occupied by a mobile cafe.*

Lonely and isolated may well also describe the feeling gained on the traverse of these wide peaty moors, a sensation perhaps heightened by the notion ventured by John Taylor of Gloucester, a vagrant who opined that the further north he travelled the longer the miles seemed to be. There is some truth in his remark, for there was a time when northern miles were longer than southern miles. At many places north of Edale the 'old British mile', 2,428 yards instead of 1,760 yards, was still in use, which

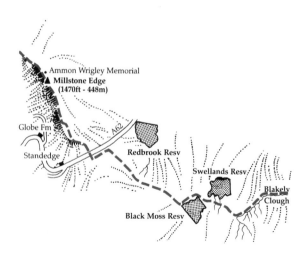

meant that you had to travel almost one and a half northern miles to cover one southern mile. What in later years came to be the standard mile was not devised until 1593, and did not appear on maps until 1675.

Cross the A635, and go down to Wessenden Head Reservoir, soon joining a service road heading northwest down the valley of Wessenden Brook. Wessenden Head Reservoir is the first of four reservoirs to occupy the valley, and the Way continues northwards to pass Wessenden Reservoir before reaching Wessenden Lodge. Cross the reservoir dam to reach a good track that contours into the notch of Shiny Brook, crossed at a weir below a waterfall.

A narrow path then leads around the eastern edge of Black Moss to gain Blakely Clough. The path becomes less prominent as it passes between Swellands and Black Moss reservoirs. After the latter, go left and shortly right at a junction with a sandy track that leads across Rocher Moss, across which Redbrook Reservoir comes into view to the north, set against the shapely wedge of Pule Hill.

The path encounters an old packhorse route before descending to Standedge Cutting where, on crossing the A62, the route passes from the area of the Peak National Park into the South Pennines. One stage could be said to have been completed, another about to begin.

2   The South Pennines

North of the Peak, the Pennine Way passes through a region now known as the South Pennines, a place that many consider a grimy, urban sprawl of industrialised towns and villages, where muck meant money and people worked long hours for a pittance. Yet nothing could be further from the truth, and, as John Gillham describes in his excellent book, South Pennines, *here are "the forgotten hills of Northern England, which... have a dramatic aura all of their own. This is wonderful walking country where history is ingrained on every pasture, from the earthworks of a Roman fort to the crumbling farmstead high on the hill".*

This is a land of dramatic scenery, brought to fame by a host of writers and poets, including the Brontë sisters, Ted Hughes, appointed poet laureate in 1984, and Ammon Wrigley, son of Saddleworth. It is a setting upon which generations of Lancashire and Yorkshire folk have lavished affection and enthusiasm, sought respite from their daily toil, and, no doubt, started new generations; and as vibrant today, perhaps more so, as it ever was, but an area much neglected by walkers with only the honeypots of the Lake District and the Yorkshire Dales in mind.

Yet the studious will find a wealth of walking, and of

social, economic and industrial heritage. If it can inspire great writers and poets, it can inspire us all. Pennine Wayfarers have no choice in the matter; between the Dark Peak and the Yorkshire Dales, the South Pennines have you at their mercy. But be assured, it will not be a painful experience.

As the Pennine Way forges northwards, the transition from the bleak moorland experience of the South Pennines to the more fecund greenness of the Yorkshire Dales becomes more pronounced, but quite where one ends and the other begins is both difficult to determine and academic. Logically, it could be argued that the Yorkshire Dales begin at the boundary of the national park, but that would lump in with the South Pennines section landscapes and villages, like Thornton-in-Craven, that have an obviously closer affinity with the Dales. Since the distinction is a point of convenience only, this section will end at the gritstone villages of Ickornshaw and Cowling, just north of Ickornshaw Moor, beyond which the change in the landscape begins to take effect.

Standedge to Hebden Bridge

15 miles (24km)

Progress from Standedge is hallmarked by high moors and gritstone summits, and punctuated by trans-Pennine roads and reservoirs that serve the needs of flanking conurbations. There used to be a pale greyness that pervaded much of the landscape, penetrated by the spectre of weary sunlight that, ever seeking to enliven the scene, probed the acres of heather and cotton grass, the tors and gritstone crags, the shy mill villages and the tight, wooded valleys.

Here still lie the images that moved Glyn Hughes to write Millstone Grit, *an evocative account of life in the north of England. Now, as Hughes's romanticised brutalities of the Industrial Revolution have receded, so they have been replaced by the brutalities of modern society, among which the quest for physical self-actualisation, expressed as a demand for walking opportunities and a freedom to roam these magnificent hills and moors, provides one ray of sunshine, and brings the same invaluable escapism it brought to our forefathers.*

Along the A62, just north of Little Brun Clough Reservoir, cross the road opposite a car park to a sandy cart track, going left for a short distance to a junction. About the same distance on, bear right near a small quarry on a clear path across rough pastures heading up the Standedge Ridge on a signposted path to Millstone Edge, on which the weathered gritstone rocks and boulders provide an intriguing photographic diversion. Although Millstone Edge falls significantly towards Castleshaw Upper Reservoir in the valley to the west, the "edge" is more a jumble of boulders than a pronounced rim.

The top of Millstone Edge is marked by a trig pillar, not far from which is a memorial to Ammon Wrigley (1861-1946), born in Saddleworth, and a poet whose works reflect a great love of his native countryside.

A good path now heads on to Northern Rocher, the last of the escarpment's outcrops, beyond which it crosses the grass and heather of Oldgate Moss to reach the A640 (Rochdale-Huddersfield) trans-Pennine highway, at an old packhorse trail.

Like many trans-Pennine roads, the A640 has its origin in the time of the packhorse trains. Later, during the 18th century, its use increased when the turnpike roads were set up and run as profit-making businesses that tapped into the essential cross-Pennine commerce of the era.

Across the road, the Way heads north-west, rising steadily towards the end of a wall on the skyline ahead. Keep on beside the wall over Rapes Hill, after which the Windy Hill mast comes into view in the middle distance. A slight dip to cross Readycon Dean provides a fine view of its reservoir, before the Way rises again to pass the trig pillar on White Hill, a comforting, grassy summit that contrasts markedly with its surroundings.

Once across White Hill, the route heads north-north-west to Green Hole Hill, and along gravelly Axletree Edge, from where it descends to another

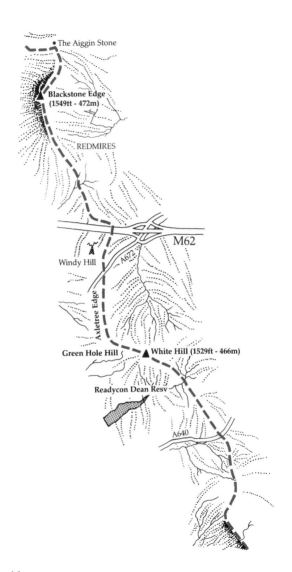

The Aiggin Stone

Blackstone Edge
(1549tt - 472m)

REDMIRES

M62

Windy Hill

A672

Axletree Edge

Green Hole Hill ▲ **White Hill (1529ft - 466m)**

Readycon Dean Resv

A640

former turnpike road, the A672, bringing with it the constant, boring drone of speeding traffic on the M62 trans-Pennine motorway, now visible ahead.

With a desire for better things putting a spring in your stride, speed on across the motorway, which is spanned by a massive airy footbridge constructed to carry the Pennine Way.

From the motorway bridge, go west (left) and then north-west heading directly for Blackstone Edge across haggard, archetypal moorland that preyed heavily on the sensibilities of the early travellers to this region.

Celia Fiennes (1662-1741), granddaughter of the first viscount Saye and Sele, travelled extensively throughout England between 1685 and 1703, recording her travels in her journal, published as a definitive edition in 1947 as The Journeys of Celia Fiennes. *This was the first comprehensive survey of the country since the days of Camden, and is notable for the perception it reveals. Blackstone Edge, she wrote, was "noted all over England for a dismal high precipice and steep in the ascent and descent on either end; it's a very moorish ground all about and even just at the top, tho' so high that you travel on a Causey, which is very troublesome as it's a moist ground, so as is usual on these high hills they stagnate the aire and hold mist and raines almost perpetually".*

Daniel Defoe (1660-1731), among his 560 books, pamphlets and journals included a vivid first-hand account of a tour throughout Britain in which he relates how the area around Blackstone Edge was so awe-inspiring that it made his horses uneasy and frightened the dog. He also managed to encounter snow here in August, but that was in 1724; it wouldn't happen now; would it? – though those who experienced the blizzard on Cross Fell in June 1993 may have a differing view.

The highest point of Blackstone Edge is a trig pillar perched on top of an enormous boulder, with an extensive view east across Yorkshire and west to the mill towns of East Lancashire. All around the scene is one of enormous gritstone boulders and small cliffs, while immediately below, the jumble of rocks has attracted the name "Robin Hood's Bed". Robin Hood, of course, is forever associated with Sherwood Forest, but he was a universal folk hero in the Middle Ages. Some opinions suggest he was also a moss trooper; if so, he would have found the many nooks and crannies of these moors ideal for his nefarious purposes.

The Way continues northwards from Blackstone Edge, heading for rather easier walking conditions, but first it encounters an enigma in the form of the so-called Roman road.

The earliest suggestion that the road might be Roman comes only a year after Defoe rode along it, with subsequent opinions supporting or rejecting the view. The controversy stems from the way the road is constructed and paved. It has many features that could be Roman, and it certainly could have linked the Roman forts of Manchester with York or Ilkley. Most informed modern opinion sees it as a packhorse causey. That it was used as a medieval packhorse route is not in question; there are records from as early as the 13th century which support this fact. In 1291, Richard de Radeclive and Hugh Elland were granted consent to levy custom for two years on goods for sale carried over "Blacksteynegge".

Where the Pennine Way meets the Roman road will be found the Aiggin Stone (pronounced Ai-jin), a single standing stone inscribed with a Latin cross and the initials I.T.. Although there is nothing to identify its purpose, it was probably an old guide post. From time to time the ancient post gets knocked over, but the Pennine Way Project Team invariably see that it is restored.

Go down the Roman road for a short distance until you intercept Broad Head Drain, an obvious man-made leat, and then follow this northwards to meet the Halifax road (A58), near the White House Inn.

Turn right at the A58 and just beyond the White House Inn leave the road, left, on a surfaced track that now makes for good, level progress as it ambles onward into reservoirland, passing three reservoirs, Blackstone Edge, Light Hazzles and Warland amid a wide expanse of heather-clad moorland that closes in a little after passing Warland Reservoir.

The reservoirs were built around the beginning of the 19th century to provide water for the Rochdale Canal, which opened in 1804.

After passing Warland Reservoir, the Way follows the Warland Drain, another leat which collects water from the many feeder streams. When the drain turns sharply right (GR964220), leave it for a well-defined path heading slightly to the right of the bouldery hump of Coldwell Hill.

On the approach to Coldwell Hill attention will begin to focus on the conspicuous pinnacle of Stoodley Pike on the northern horizon.

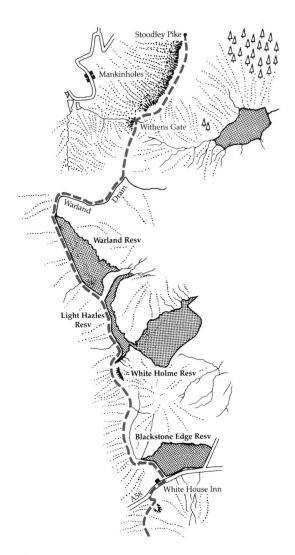

Stoodley Pike

Mankinholes

Withens Gate

Drain

Warland

Warland Resv

Light Hazles
Resv

White Holme Resv

Blackstone Edge Resv

A58

White House Inn

An easy descent leads from Coldwell Hill to meet the Calderdale Way at Withens Gate, from where walkers who want to stop at this stage can descend to Mankinholes and Todmorden. Otherwise, from Withens Gate it is a straightforward walk up the crest of Higher Moor to reach Stoodley Pike.

The history of the Pike is rather more fascinating than its appearance. It was the exile of Napoleon to Elba in 1814 that prompted the construction of a 'congratulatory' monument to peace on the site now occupied by Stoodley Pike. Unfortunately, Napoleon escaped and returned to France in March 1815, overthrew the restored monarchy, and began his reign of a Hundred Days. Work on the monument was halted, but restarted after Napoleon's defeat at the Battle of Waterloo on 18 June 1815.

In 1854, coinciding with the outbreak of the Crimean War, the monument collapsed and the present tower was built two years later, though it needed repair again in 1918. Now it is one of the best-known landmarks in the Pennines, and a tantalising target for northbound Wayfarers.

From Stoodley Pike, the Way now runs eastwards to a squeeze stile in a wall, beyond which it goes left over a ladder stile and then runs down past a prominent outcropping of gritstone known as the Doe Stones to reach a track junction near Swillington Farm. Cross the lateral track here and descend to a gate. Keep ahead, beside a wall, to a step stile on the right. Cross the stile and over the next field to another stile, and here keep on to reach the farm access to Lower Rough Head Farm. Go left around the farm and follow a delightful track down into Callis Wood.

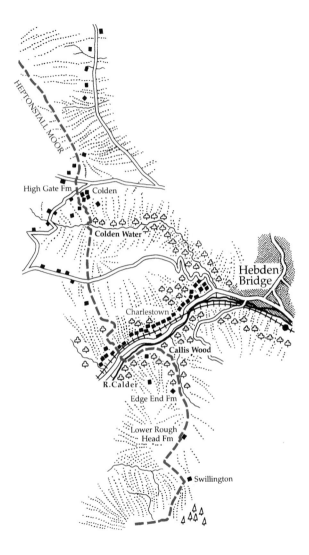

Stay on the main track to reach a lower track circling left to a farm. Leave the main track here and go down through sparse woodland to rejoin the farm access. Ignore tempting footpaths on the right, and go on down the main track to a bridge over the Rochdale Canal and the River Calder.

The centre of Hebden Bridge is most easily and pleasantly reached by a canal-side stroll as far as Black Pit Lock, where the canal is left and the town centre reached via Holme Street.

Hebden Bridge is a traditional mill and foundry town snugly embraced in the valley where Hebden Water joins the River Calder. It is a busy, bustling little town with a proud heritage and a friendly welcome. If you are looking for stark, grimy industrial banality, you will not find it here; modern Hebden is bright and alive.

It was here in 1841 that Bramwell, the black sheep of the Brontë family, came as clerk-in-charge of Luddenden Foot, a small railway station 4 miles (6km) away on the line to Sowerby Bridge. His family hoped he might find a new lease of life, but, with little traffic to deal with, he was often to be found in the nearby Lord Nelson, and later in the White Horse in Hebden Bridge.

Hebden Bridge to Ponden

11 miles (17.5km)

As it presses on from Hebden Bridge and the Calder valley, the Pennine Way climbs steeply for a short while before loping across Heptonstall Moor to reach tranquil Walshaw Dean and the celebrated Brontë Moors of Haworth. Here there is fine walking across open, elevated moorlands dotted with numerous blue-eyed reservoirs, the whole probed by the fingers of pleasant valleys each with its share of attractive villages and hamlets. The lingering memories of the industrial past encountered in the Calder valley are soon forgotten as you rise above the denes and begin to stretch out along this memorable section.

Leave the A646 at a signpost sending the Way along a side road known as Underbank Avenue, passing beneath a railway bridge on a line that served the former Lancashire and Yorkshire Railway. A footpath climbs past cottages and the ruins of a chapel with a small graveyard, with the view back across the valley to Stoodley Pike improving with every step.

From the ruin, contour right, across the hillside, rising steadily through patchy heather to reach steps near a small cascade. Now the Way passes round farm buildings, and by a walled trackway to a junction. Here, go left to a gap in a wall on the right, from where the route finally sets off north again in earnest.

There is clear evidence throughout this early section of the way in which the early farming landscape was parcelled into enclosures. Around Heptonstall this would have occurred over a long period, most recently during the latter part of the 18th century. But it is a mistake to think that this period and the early 19th century marked the earliest times when the open field system of farming was abandoned. Much earlier than this, notably during the early 12th century, when the original church was built, large tracts of farm land would already have been enclosed between hedge-rows, producing rows of narrow small fields. However, the break up of the former massive fields, motivated by higher profits and less piecemeal land use, accelerated at the end of the 18th century.

The Way presses on over fields, crosses Badger Lane and Pry Hill to descend through heather and bilberry into Colden Clough, a pleasant woodland dene in which Colden Water and its bankside gritstone boulders is a tempting place to rest. Cross Colden Water by a stone packhorse bridge, where both the Pennine Way and the Calderdale Way meet, and climb steeply, trending left on a walled track that leads around a farm, keeping on to the hamlet of Colden beside the Blackshaw Head-Heptonstall road.

The path leads on past Long High Top Farm and Mount Pleasant Farm from where it follows a roughly north-westwards course on to Clough Head Hill and the featureless wild, open spaces of Heptonstall Moor. The highest point hereabouts is Standing Stone Hill, but the Way keeps north of this, descending slightly and overlooking Hebden Dale and Hardcastle Crags. Northwards, it is possible to pick out Walshaw Dean Reservoirs, an objective soon to be reached.

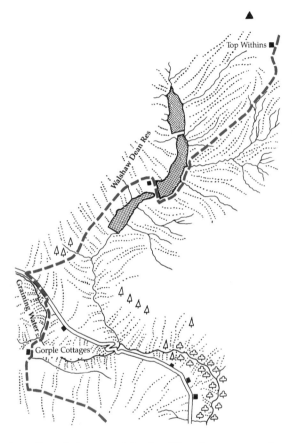

A wall and fence guide the Way down towards Gorple Lower Reservoir descending, right, past Gorple Cottages and across the reservoir access road, into a rocky hollow where Reaps Water and the delightful Graining Water meet. Two wooden footbridges cross these streams, beyond which a path climbs to the Brierfield-Hebden Bridge road.

Turn left along the road to a surfaced waterworks road on the right (GR947324), to reach Walshaw Dean, climbing across the flanks of Greave Pasture to reach the first of the three reservoirs in the valley. [At the time of writing, there is a temporary diversion at this point, turning the Way right before the first reservoir, and following its east bank to reach the dam of the middle reservoir.]

The official Way crosses the dam of the middle reservoir and turns left over a footbridge to continue through rhododendrons on the opposite side. Shortly after the bridge spanning Black Clough, the Way branches right and begins its ascent on to Withins Height. The climb is mainly through heather on a causey path constructed by Calderdale Council, though the skill with which it has been laid could fool you into thinking it had been there for much longer.

Although attention will be focused ahead, the retrospective view across the three reservoirs and south to the monument of Stoodley Pike more than justifies the odd pause for breath.

As the watershed is crossed you gaze down on the landscape that so inspired the Brontë sisters, and the farm that many consider became Wuthering Heights in the imagination of Emily Brontë. Anyone seeking a shrine will be disappointed with Top Withins. A plaque erected by the Brontë Society makes clear that the buildings bore no resemblance to Wuthering Heights, though there must have been some imprint of this remarkable, austere landscape in Emily's thoughts when she wrote her book. The farmstead was occupied until the 1930s. The real location is now thought to have been High Sunderland Hall, near Halifax.

The Brontës were a uniquely-gifted family who lived in the emotionally-repressed conditions of Victorian times. Anne, Charlotte and Emily are the most renowned, but they had two other sisters, Maria and Elizabeth, who died in childhood, and a brother, Bramwell, a man who squandered his talents with alcohol and proved to be a great disappointment to the family.

The girls were born in Thornton to a father who was an Irish clergyman, and a Cornish mother, Maria, who died of cancer in 1821. After their mother's death the girls were taken into the care of an austere aunt from whom their only escape lay in writing and exploring the countryside around their home in Haworth.

The way down to Top Withins is along a clear, paved causey, continuing above the valley of South Dean Beck, a place popular with the Brontë sisters, and across tussocky moorland and then through banks of heather to reach Upper Heights Cottage. Note the 1761 date and mysterious face above the doorway.

Immediately after Upper Heights, turn left to reach Lower Heights Farm, continuing gently down on a broad track through heather until the Way leaves it and goes left along the Brontë Way. This is a wide, grassy drove road flanked by walls, over the top of which you gaze down on the village of Stanbury and Lower Leith Reservoir. As it descends, the path veers right to Buckley Green. Just before reaching Buckley Green go right, on a minor back road, and then sharp left along another broad track leading to a row of cottages, near which the route crosses a signposted stile on the right to access a descending flight of steps often running with water. They lead to a pathway between walls heading down to Rush Isles Farm, descending to Ponden Reservoir. The Way keeps to the left of Ponden Reservoir and leads round to Ponden Hall.

Walkers in need of refreshment or an overnight stay should, on reaching Ponden Reservoir, keep ahead across its dam to reach the Colne-Haworth road. Then turn right to go down to Haworth, which is about 2 miles (3.5 km) distant. There is also B&B and a campsite at Ponden Hall. A more direct route to Haworth is from Top Withins, leaving the official route of the Way just after the ruins and branching right to go down to the Brontë Falls on a well-established path, beyond which another path runs down to Haworth.

Ponden Hall was originally built in 1680, but restored in 1801. It was later claimed to be the inspiration for Emily Brontë's Thrushcross Grange.

Follow the track past Ponden Hall and contour above the reservoir, then turn sharply right downhill. A bridge at the head of the reservoir enables the Way to reach the Colne-Haworth road.

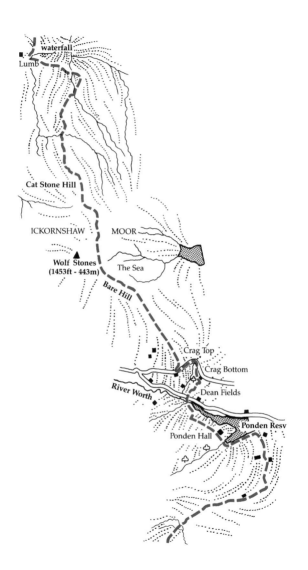

waterfall

Lumb

Cat Stone Hill

ICKORNSHAW

MOOR

Wolf Stones
(1453ft - 443m)

The Sea

Bare Hill

Crag Top

Crag Bottom

River Worth

Dean Fields

Ponden Resv

Ponden Hall

Ponden to Cowling

3½ miles (6 km)

On reaching the Colne-Haworth road, the Pennine Way goes left (west) to a ladder stile on the right, over which it heads up a grassy path above Dean Clough. Now pass through a gap in a wall and head up the pastures of Dean Fields, using old gateposts as guides, going left along a track just after a ruined barn. Soon this becomes a walled track which is abandoned, left, after another set of old gateposts. Follow the line of a wall to reach a lane, turning left here and round the head of Dean Clough.

After crossing Dean Clough stay on the lane to Old Crag Bottom Farm, turning right there, leaving the lane to climb to the spectacular viewpoint of Crag Top, which embraces the Worth valley below, its reservoirs and the rising domes of the Brontë Moors.

From Crag Top the Way heads north-west over Thornton Hill, rising in company with a wall and/or a fence and wall through the familiar South Pennine landscape of bilberry, marsh and finally broad expanses of heather. Beyond Old Bess Hill, where the wall and fence come to an end, the Way presses on up a broad ridge above Keighley Moor Reservoir to flank a boggy area and a small peaty pool known as The Sea, and over the slopes of Wolf Stones.

The top of Wolf Stones is marked by a trig pillar, but before reaching it bear right, heading northwards, heading for a stile over a fence. Beyond the fence the Way enters the ancient district of Craven, of which Skipton is the capital, but which is here represented by the gritstone-slabbed expanse of Ickornshaw Moor.

The Way takes a rather meandering, but flagged, course over Ickornshaw Moor, descending from the highest point north-east of Wolf Stones to cross Cat Stone Hill, a name that recalls the former presence here of wildcats, which, like the wolves, may have occupied the summit and shoulders of Wolf Stones Hill before the 17th century.

A cairned path leads on across High End Lowe, which is a fine vantage point that takes in Bouls-worth Hill to the south and, to the north-east, two prominent monuments, Wainman's Pinnacle and Lund's Tower.

Wainman's Pinnacle is a needle-like obelisk on a massive gritstone outcrop on the edge of Earl Crag, the origins of which historians cannot agree. There is a claim that Lady Amcotts, one of the Wainman family, had it constructed in memory of her husband who was killed at war. Others suggest that it marks the Battle of Waterloo, and was constructed by Richard Wainman to the memory of his son, killed in the battle.

Lund's Tower, also known as Sutton Pinnacle, is a folly constructed by James Lund of Malsis Hall to commemorate Queen Victoria's Golden Jubilee.

Beyond High End Lowe, the Way goes down a path beside a wall, bearing sharp left at a stile as the ground steepens near Further Dean Hole. It soon crosses Andrew Gutter by a footbridge to pass Higher Dean Hole and a number of ruined farms before passing round the waterfall at Lumb Head.

After that, walled tracks and a green lane lead down to Lower Summer House, then by stiles, walls and pastures to reach the A6068 between Ickornshaw and Cowling.

On this approach to Ickornshaw, a sign diverts walkers from the marked Pennine Way across a stream to Ickornshaw village, directing the Way left along the A6068 to the Black Bull Inn. On the nearside of the inn a signposted route heads north to the lane at Ickornshaw, then right, to the church.

Cowling, a former industrial village, was the birthplace of Philip Snowden PC (1864-1937), First Viscount of Snowden, a right wing politician and Chancellor of the Exchequer in 1924 and 1929-31. A rather less worthy distinction was his role in disarming Britain's defences and his lack of support for those who saw what was really afoot in pre-World War II Germany.

3   The Yorkshire Dales

One of the many delights of the Pennine Way is the variety brought by the differing landscapes en route. Often the distinction is no more than a subtle change of hue in the vegetation, for example, a move from tussock grass to heather, bog cotton or bilberry. Or it may be a slight change in the way the land falls to the river valley, denoting geological changes beneath the surface that offer more, or less, resistance to the processes of erosion. Or it may be simply a change in the colour of the bare rocks that swell from the heather, peat and bracken, or in the stones that compose the ubiquitous drystone walls.

At other times the change is much more noticeable, and so it is as the Way advances from the wild landscapes of the Peak and South Pennines into the Yorkshire Dales. Quite where one ends and the other begins may well be a matter of geomorphology. But it is not until Lothersdale, where the first glimpse comes of the limestone for which the Dales are especially renowned, or along the Aire, near Skipton and at Gargrave, that the characteristic Dales landscape starts really to impress itself.

Between the Peak and the South Pennines you might be forgiven for failing to register any significant change in the landscape, but between the

South Pennines and the Yorkshire Dales the distinction has major impact, and with it comes a real sense that you are making progress along the Way. Those of us who love the great peaty swathes of the Peak, and the high, bleak moorlands and gritty valleys of the South Pennines move onwards with reluctance and expectation. Sorry to see those swelling hillsides slip away, we are happy to be marching into a new chapter of the Pennine tale.

Once Ickornshaw Moor is crossed, the Way heads promptly for the softer scenery of Craven and Airedale, threading tenuous trails through a verdant and pastoral landscape to Malham before sweeping across Penyghent to Ribblesdale. Beyond that lie Hawes, Great Shunner Fell and the splendours of Swaledale before it finally takes its leave of the Dales at Tan Hill, on the very northern edge of the Yorkshire Dales National Park. Beyond that it moves into North Pennine country and the raw magnificence of Upper Teesdale.

Cowling to Thornton-in-Craven

6 miles (10km)

Beyond the A6068, the Way slips easily down to Ickornshaw, where the Black Bull is a real temptation, and passes the church before pressing on northwards along the lane to Middleton. Gill Lane leads to Gill Bridge, spanning a beck of the same name that boasts a fine dash of deciduous woodland. After the bridge, turn left then right along a track, climbing hill pastures on easy pathways to the derelict High Stubbings Farm, beyond which the Way reaches Cowling Hill Lane.

Turn right here, then left, along a lane to Over House, staying on the lane until at a sharp right bend the route quits the lane by a stile into more pastures, descending to cross Surgill Beck before rising to Woodhead Farm. Just beyond the farm the path forks. Take the right branch heading steeply down beside a wall to the village of Lothersdale. On reaching the village road, turn right, and over a bridge into the village.

The delightful village of Lothersdale comes into view after Woodhead Farm, though from such a distance little is learned of its charms until the largely-hidden village is actually reached. Its stone terraced cottages and tall mill chimney tell a tale of industrial heritage that may cause the curious to think about staying overnight in Lothersdale. The village's seclusion, sheltered under the

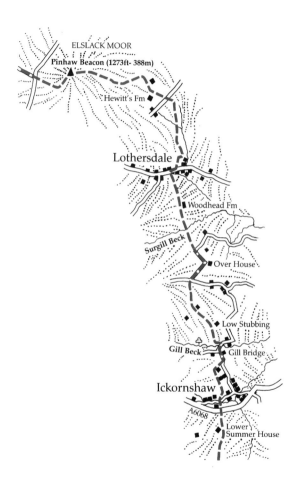

ELSLACK MOOR

Pinhaw Beacon (1273ft- 388m)

Hewitt's Fm

Lothersdale

Woodhead Fm

Surgill Beck

Over House

Low Stubbing

Gill Beck   Gill Bridge

Ickornshaw

A6068

Lower
Summer House

bastion of Pinhaw Beacon to the north, sustains the impression that time has passed it by. A short way east stands Stone Gappe, an isolated mansion where Charlotte Brontë lived as governess for a few months.

Turn left after the Hare and Hounds Inn in Lothersdale, through a farmyard, and on through more enclosed meadowland on good paths above Stansfield Beck. Cross White Hill Lane and take to a concrete access track as far as Hewitts Farm. Leave the track here and cross a wall, heading uphill until, after a stile over the intake wall, sandy paths through heather lead westward across Elslack Moor to Pinhaw and its beacon. The summit, marked by a trig pillar and a small cairn, stands at 1,273 feet (388m), and affords a spectacular view.

To the south, Wainman's Pinnacle and Lund's Tower on the edge of Earl Crag rise above the green and heathered flanks of Ickornshaw Moor, while across the low-lying lands of the Aire and the Ribble the horizon is etched with familiar landmarks, from the distinctive flat top of Ingleborough to the moors and hills of Wharfedale.

Across Pinhaw, the Way passes an old quarry to a road junction, crossing into Clogger Lane, which is bound for Elslack village. After about 600yds/m, leave the lane and, keeping to the left of the wall on your left, press on downhill through meadows and through the farmyard at Brown House Farm, before rising onwards and easily to pass beneath an old railway bridge before ascending lanes into Thornton-in-Craven.

Thornton is as charming as its setting, in spite of the

incongruous notes sounded by the A56 and the B6252. The village commands lovely views of the valley, and is, like Lothersdale, a gem among the rich, green hills that amply and capably prelude the delights of the Yorkshire Dales.

It was at Thornton that an English parliamentary soldier known as Honest John Lambert (1619-84), found his bride and married her. He was born near Settle, and on the outbreak of the Civil War in 1641 became a captain in Fairfax's army, leading the cavalry at the Battle of Marston Moor. He commanded under Cromwell, at Dunbar in 1650, and pursued Charles II to Worcester in 1651, there commanding the troops on the east bank of the River Severn. He helped to install Cromwell as Protector, but opposed his desire to become king. Later, after becoming Member of Parliament for Pontefract, he was looked on as the leader of the extreme Republican Party. He and his officers virtually governed the country until his plans were frustrated by General Monck. He was tried in 1662, and kept prisoner on Drake's Island until his death.

Thornton-in-Craven to Malham

10¹/₂ miles (17km)

The stretch of the Pennine Way between Thornton-in-Craven and Malham is a gentle interlude of easy walking, a time to reflect on what has gone before, and to anticipate the limestone wonderland ahead. This section will be the source of many pleasant memories of gently rolling hillsides, sylvan glades, canalside strolling, charming villages and riparian rambling as the Way presses ever northward to the thrill of Malham, Horton-in-Ribblesdale, Hawes and beyond.

Leave Thornton northward along Cam Lane, a narrow surfaced lane that leads past terraced cottages, and soon becomes a rutted track, keeping to the left of Old Cote Farm. Route-finding is not a problem as the Way traverses sloping fields before easing downwards to cross Langber Beck, east of Langber Farm. Throughout this section the going is firm, and the scenery is most agreeable. A stone bridge spans Langber Beck, beyond which the Way crosses the shoulder of Langber Hill to drop to meet the Leeds and Liverpool Canal, which it now follows to East Marton.

The Leeds and Liverpool Canal is, at 127 miles (203km), one of Britain's longest navigable waterways and was once a busy thoroughfare thronged with narrowboats pulled by horses. Like most canals, however, its life was brief, and ended with the coming of the railways which made these waterways less competitive. By the 1920s, the life had gone

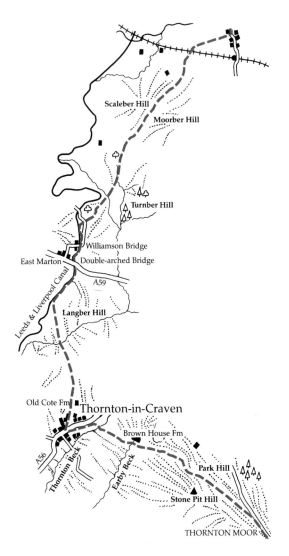

Scaleber Hill

Moorber Hill

Turnber Hill

Williamson Bridge

East Marton   Double-arched Bridge

Leeds & Liverpool Canal

A59

Langber Hill

Old Cote Fm

Thornton-in-Craven

Brown House Fm

A56

Thornton Beck

Earby Beck

Park Hill

Stone Pit Hill

THORNTON MOOR

from the canal, until the modern penchant for leisure cruising gave this, and others, a new lease of life. The Leeds and Liverpool Canal at East Marton is arguably the most beautiful stretch of the waterway.

The Pennine Way follows the towpath northwards, passing beneath the busy A59, the only blemish on a particularly beautiful stretch of canal, dappled with sunlight filtered through beech and sycamore and enlivened by the bright colours of the narrowboats. Stay along the towpath as far as Williamson Bridge, then bear right, up a bank to reach a lane.

Follow the lane for a few hundred yds/m, then take a path across a field (on the right, signposted) that abridges a corner before debouching on the lane once more. Little more than 100yds/m along the lane, you reach a bridge adjacent to Trenet Laithe, where the route rises into hill pastures that form the north-western slopes of Turnber Hill. A slight descent leads to Crickle Beck, after which the Way moves away for a short distance, rejoining Crickle Beck east of Newton Grange Farm, before finally ascending Scaleber Hill.

Scaleber Hill is no giant among mountains, but from its top the view widens dramatically to take in the Aire valley, green with lush, walled and hedge-rowed meadows, dotted with farms, barns and cottages. To the north-east St Andrew's Church and the grey village of Gargrave dominate the dale, serving as a spur, for just beyond lies the boundary of the Yorkshire Dales National Park and the purlieu of limestone country.

After crossing Scaleber Hill, the Way descends into

72

the wide Aire valley, soon reaching a surfaced lane and following this across the Leeds-Kendal railway. About 50yds/m after the railway bridge, turn right across fields and by a squeeze stile reach the outskirts of Gargrave. Turn right, through a gate, and left to reach the middle of the village. At the end of the road, the Way crosses the River Aire.

Gargrave used to be the old central parish of Craven, and was once a market town. In medieval times, the country-side around Gargrave was rich and fertile, and regularly devastated by Scottish reivers, with only the church, named after their patron saint, being spared their attentions.

In 1730, the daughter of the local vicar commented that one of her childhood pleasures was listening to the bells of the packhorses as they travelled the lanes across unenclosed arable fields that were divided into strips, called 'lands'. Another local diarist, William Paley of Settle, observed that on 27 April 1826 power looms were attacked by an armed mob of Luddites.

Over the bridge and across the main road, the Way goes north by a side road, past the village hall. Here the route takes to a quieter lane that crosses the Leeds and Liverpool Canal. When this lane turns to the right, keep on a narrow lane which passes round Gargrave House, beside a wood.

After the wood the lane is abandoned by the Way, which begins a waymarked and complicated route across high pastureland, slipping, at a hill crest wall, into the Yorkshire Dales National Park on Steeple Hill. Down across the fields of Eshton Moor, the Way rejoins the River Aire just south of

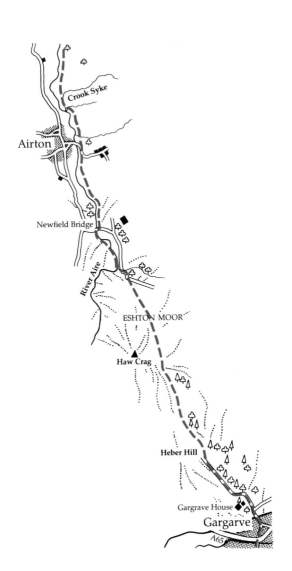

Crook Syke

Airton

Newfield Bridge

River Aire

ESHTON MOOR

Haw Crag

Heber Hill

Gargrave House

Gargarve

A65

Newfield Hall. Cross the Aire by a footbridge and press on along its true right bank (west) to meet a lane at Newfield Bridge. Having recrossed the river here, the Way now hurries northwards, never far from the river, passing the village of Airton, and keeping on to reach a lane at Hanlith.

Airton, Hanlith and Malham, a short way ahead, are villages founded by the Angles, while nearby Kirkby Malham owes its origin to the Danes. Man has inhabited these upper reaches of Airedale since Mesolithic times, a period when hunting was abandoned for a lifestyle that began by exploiting the resources of the forests and ended with the introduction of farming about 5,000BC. In much more recent times linen weavers lived at Airton, and in the latter half of the 18th century the manufacture of cotton was introduced, with the new mills often being built on the sites of the former manorial corn mills; certainly this was the case at Airton, Malham and Kirkby Malham.

The name of Hanlith comes from a personal name, and means the hillslope of Hagena. It is a tiny village dominated by Hanlith Hall which for many years was the home of an ancient Malhamdale family, the Serjeantsons.

John Dower lived at nearby Kirkby Malham during the last war. While living here, he was commissioned to prepare a report on national parks in England and Wales, which was published in 1945, and augured the development of national parks. To this day, the offices of the Countryside Commission in Cheltenham are named in his memory.

The riverside route by-passes the centre of Airton, but, if time permits, it is worth making the short detour to visit the Friends' Meeting House and the squatter's house on the village green. The squatter's house is a relic from the 17th century when it was possible for a homeless person to build a house on common ground.

The Way keeps on through the parklands of Hanlith Hall, now with the gleaming wall of Malham Cove rising in the distance and marking the start of the Great Scar Limestone scenery. North of Hanlith, where the Way uses the road for a short distance, the route follows a pleasant and flat riverside path into the village of Malham.

Malham today is a tourist mecca. Its origins go back at least to AD700 when it was a simple settlement around a village green. Four hundred years later, the village stream became the boundary of lands owned by Fountains Abbey and Bolton Priory, and so the village was effectively cut into two, a dichotomy of interest that was to survive until Henry VIII's dissolution of the monasteries. During the 19th and 20th centuries Malham was a place of mines and mills, in common with much of the dale.

Whatever its history, whatever the indignities to which popularity now puts it, the beauty of Malham never pales. The sight of Malham Cove, a former waterfall of dramatic proportions, is certain to set any heart racing, while the maw of Gordale Scar is simply astounding. Even so, Thomas Gray, the poet, found the place 'dreary'. William and Dorothy Wordsworth, who came here at the beginning of the 19th century, rested at Gordale 'for several hours', and presumably found it to their liking.

Malham to Horton-in-Ribblesdale

14 miles (22.5km)

Between Malham and Ribblesdale the Pennine Way gets to grips with two of the many fine summits of Craven limestone country, Fountains Fell and Penyghent, and promises Wayfarers a day of quality walking that should not be underestimated. There is an escape route from below the prow of Penyghent that will lead more speedily into Ribblesdale. Leaving the early morning tranquillity of Malham can often be a wrench, but one made easier by the sheer magnetism of that great wall of limestone awaiting inspection only a short walk away.

The Way leaves the village along Cove Road (signposted to Malham Tarn), keeping left when the road divides near the stone bridge, and passing the cluster of buildings at Town Head. One is Calamine House, and it was here that quantities of zinc mined from the surrounding hills were stored prior to shipment to the brass foundries of the Midlands.

A short way on, leave the road to gain a gravel path (signposted) on the right that heads alongside ash-lined Malham Beck for the conspicuous wall of Malham Cove. A short way before the base of the cliffs, the Pennine Way ascends a long flight of stony steps on the left, but it is worth taking a few minutes to go forward to the spot under the cove where Malham Beck emerges.

The setting is awe-inspiring. The span of the cove is some

Field Centre

Malham Tarn

Tarn Foot

Malham Cove

Malham Beck

Malham

Gordale Beck

Kirkby Malham

River Aire

Hanlith Bridge

200yds/m, with grassy ledges trying vainly to meet in the middle. The height of the cove wall is 70yds/m, topped above by layers of outcropping that add even more height. Lower down, the slopes below the cove walls are host to one of Britain's most beautiful wild flowers, Jacob's Ladder (Polemonium caeruleum), which grows on scree and rocky ledges, and was first observed at Malham in 1671. The name Jacob's Ladder probably derives from the fact that the plant has rows of rung-like leaflets, and so recalls the biblical tale in Genesis.

From the bottom of the cliff wall Malham Beck flows out from a small pool, but cave exploration at this point is frustrated by a low underground passage, sealing the mysteries of the inner workings of these cave systems. Logically, the water which flows from the cliff should be that issuing from Malham Tarn, which disappears not far away at Malham Sinks, but this is not so. Tests were carried out in the 1870s and about 30 years ago, which clearly demonstrated that the water from Malham Tarn issues at Aire Head, 700yds/m south of Malham village. It must follow then that within the cave systems of Malham Cove two underground streams actually cross over one another in a complex hydrology.

Return to the ascending flight of steps and climb them. Frequent pauses and looks back enable some idea to be gained of the farming history of this remarkable place.

Many of the drystone walls date from the time of the Enclosure Acts, about 200 years ago. Above and to the right of Malham Beck can be picked out a series of horizontal ledges, known as lynchets. These were constructed almost 1,000 years ago to bring more land into cultivation on the steeper slopes. Even older, though not easy to see in morning light, are several Celtic field boundaries built at the time of Christ. The limestone pavement is a kind of geological crazy paving. The fissures between the blocks of limestone are called grykes, while the blocks themselves are known as clints. Within the grykes the botanist will find a rich array of limestone-loving plants, protected from the sun and the nibbling attentions of ever-hungry sheep.

At the top of the steps, cross a stile and bear right across one of the finest expanses of limestone pavement in Britain. As a warning to those who venture too close to the edge, this can be very slippery when wet. Within minutes the route reaches the dry valley of Watlowes, which once held the waters that flowed over the lip of the cove.

Here the Pennine Way once crossed the dry valley through delightful limestone outcrops to Malham Tarn; now a new line is taken. From the top of Malham Cove go left along the dry Watlowes valley. This signposted route clambers through easy rocky gorges, passes the base of a dry water-fall and climbs by stone steps to circle round to the top of the fall, and continues through more limestone scenery of the highest order, before emerging at Water Sinks, a spot where the water from Malham Tarn literally sinks from sight. Beyond this the unenclosed road that lies roughly along the line of the North Craven Fault, is reached.

Here there is a demarcation that is not instantly obvious, but becomes so with a little observation. The limestone landscape of Malham allows water to sink through it, yet here there lies Malham Tarn, a massive expanse of water. Clearly, something has changed, and so it has, for the North Craven Fault marks a boundary between the limestone country to the south and a section of impermeable slate to the north on which Malham Tarn reposes. The tarn is natural, but it was extended in 1791 by Lord Ribblesdale who built a small dam to stabilise the level of the lake. The tarn and its wetlands are internationally important for wildlife and were designated a National Nature Reserve in 1992.

Cross the road and, keeping the tarn well to the left, follow its shoreline, heading north-east some distance from it, over cropped turf until the former line of the Pennine Way is met near woodland.

The scenery around Malham has been an inspiration for many, notably John Ruskin, and Charles Kingsley, who wrote part of The Water Babies *while staying as a guest of Walter Morrison at Tarn House. The grand mansion, built in 1780, and the surrounding estate are owned by the National Trust and leased to the Field Studies Council. Beyond Tarn House the Way presses on along a broad track until, just before a house, it branches right. Go through a gate and on to a green path running roughly northwards through fields and parallel with the minor road from Malham, until the path runs downhill to reach the Stainforth-Arncliffe road.*

Cross the road and go through a gate near a cattle grid and along the access road to Tennant Gill Farm. Beyond the farm, the Way begins a long pull on to Fountains Fell, following an old mine track that is occasionally wet. The top of the featureless ascent seems a long time coming, and the true high point of the fell lies off the route to the south-west amid cairns and long-abandoned coal pits.

Crossing a ridge wall the classic lines of Penyghent appear across Silverdale, and hasten the step down a rocky pathway, which in due course meets a wall which it then follows down to the Stainforth-Halton

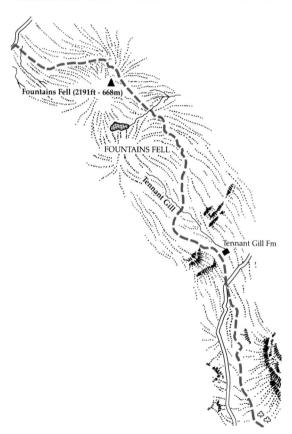

Gill road. To the left of Penyghent the distinctive shape of Ingleborough appears on the horizon. Turn left along the road and pass Rainscar until, just past a roadside parking area on the left, a track can be taken on the right to Dale Head Farm, beyond which the Way leads on to Churn Milk Pot, one of many entrances to the underground cave systems of this countryside.

From Fountains Fell, the Way has given grandstand views of Penyghent, sailing like some two-tiered galleon across the surrounding moors. With every step the bulk of Penyghent grows larger and seems more and more daunting. In the event, the ascent is not as difficult as it seems, but heavy packs and inclement weather can alter this view.

At Churn Milk Pot the Way swings northwards, targeting Penyghent. The path rises gradually across boggy moorland to a wall which shepherds the route to the base of Penyghent. On the way it passes a stile on the left over which a quick descent can be made to Brackenbottom and the sanctuary of Ribblesdale, if necessary. The way up Penyghent is never in doubt, and rises in two gigantic steps, each with a brief rocky scramble, to a final, almost level, stroll across peat and turf to the summit.

Penyghent is the lowest of Yorkshire's famous Three Peaks, and from it the other two, Ingleborough and Whernside are well seen. Its name is of Celtic origin, dating from the time of the Brigantes, one of the tribes forced into these remote regions by the Romans. Some authorities suggest that the name means the hill of the winds, while others offer the hill of the border country.

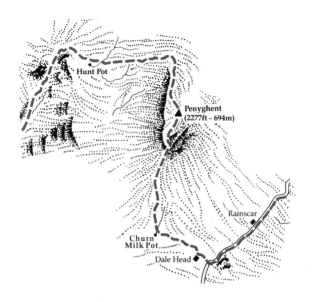

Cross the summit wall and descend a well-worn path to a sharp left turn, beyond which a steep descent leads down across the sweeping fellsides to a gate into a wide, walled lane. With time to spare a deviation northwards will quickly lead to Hull Pot, a stunning open chasm which after prolonged rain provides a spectacular waterfall. The walled lane leads back to refreshments, a warm bath or a bed that Horton-in-Ribblesdale offers.

Horton-in-Ribblesdale is rather a straggling village along the B-road from Settle to Ribblehead. It is mentioned as a farming settlement in the Domesday Book, and it was here that Henry VI came during the Wars of the Roses (1455-85) to evade his enemies.

Horton-in-Ribblesdale to Hawes

14 miles (22.5km)

From Horton, the Pennine Way loops high across the gathering grounds of the River Wharfe, bound for the distant market town of Hawes. A good stretch of the route coincides with a Roman road, while a brief interlude is spent with a more modern thoroughfare, the Dales Way, which on Cam Fell climbs out of Wharfedale en route to Ribblehead. The landscape is one of high mountain moorland and a few isolated hill farms, and provides stunning views of the high mountains of the Dales, contrasting markedly with the limestone wonderland around Malham. This is exhilarating walking across the finest Pennine scenery, and the whole section is one on which good progress can be made.

From the end of the walled track leading down from Penyghent, the Way continues along the B6479 through Horton to the northern end of the village, as far as the sharp left bend in the road where it turns to cross the River Ribble. Here, near the Crown Hotel, leave the road for an attractive walled track, Horber Scar Lane, that ascends easily across the eastern flank of Ribblesdale, heading roughly in a northerly direction.

The entrances to potholes are passed on the way, notably Sell Gill Holes and Jackdaw Hole, a clue to the presence of a labyrinth of caves and water systems beneath a landscape that has been inhabited by man since the glaciers that formed the valley retreated 10-11,000 years ago.

The early stages of the ascent are accompanied by a drystone wall, but this is abandoned at a gate, continuing along the track to another gate. Beyond this gate turn left, ascending and descending to pass around the south-western edge of Greenfield Plantation, and Old Ing Farm. Just before a gate near the farm, bear right on an old packhorse trail, and press on around Cave Hill and Fair Bottom Hill to reach boisterous Ling Gill, set in a deep, wooded limestone ravine.

This is one of many nature reserves along the Pennine Way, and a springtime trek along the Way will demonstrate why, for it plays host to a wide range of wild flowers.

Cross Ling Gill Bridge, rebuilt in 1765, according to its inscription "at the charge of the whole of West Rydeing". It is a timely reminder, perhaps, that not only does the West Riding of Yorkshire no longer exist, having disappeared in 1974, but neither does the upstart West Yorkshire, which expired in the 1984 local government reshuffle.

Beyond Ling Gill Bridge the Way meanders uphill, generally northwards until, at a junction of tracks on Cam End, it meets both the Dales Way and Cam High Road.

The origins of Cam High Road are most likely prehistoric. It was certainly used by the Romans, and later, when it acquired its present name, by packhorse traders for whom Gearstones on the B6255, Blea Moor Road, was an important staging post and overnight halt.

Beyond Gearstones, at Ribblehead, stands the massive viaduct that carries the Settle-Carlisle railway line, once

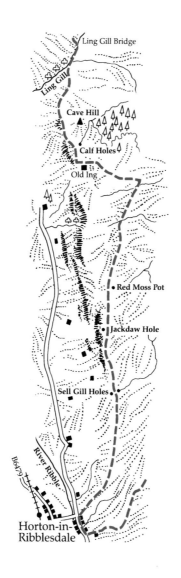

Ling Gill Bridge

Ling Gill

Cave Hill

Calf Holes

Old Ing

Red Moss Pot

Jackdaw Hole

Sell Gill Holes

River Ribble

B6479

Horton-in-Ribblesdale

threatened with closure, but saved by the dedication of a resolute group of enthusiasts. The railway, built at enormous cost both in terms of finance and of human life, is a reminder of the Midland Railway's determination to construct a route to Scotland, a determination matched only by those who much later fought to save the line. Behind the viaduct rises the great mound of Whernside, highest of the Three Peaks.

The route now continues as a straight line, rising a little, with only the deviation of the Dales Way to the right, at a cairn, to be avoided.

Walkers who want to extend their day from Horton this far will find Cam Houses, a short way down the Dales Way, an excellent high moor experience with a warm welcome and plenty of accommodation.

Keeping to the high ground, the Pennine Way presses on past the vehicle access to Cam Houses to reach Kidhow Gate. The surfaced lane from Cam Houses swings right here, through a gate, and this will provide a more consistent underfoot surface and lead directly to Hawes, though it is a little longer than the official line. This trends left along the continuing packhorse trail, here known as West Cam Road, traversing the western slopes of Dodd Fell Hill high above the deep-set valleys of Snaizeholme Beck and Widdale and on the edge of steepening ground.

The Way rises gently to Ten End, which marks the highest point of the crossing from Horton to Hawes, unless peak-bagging ambition leads across the untracked, boggy summit of Dodd Fell Hill.

Dodd Fell

Kidhow Gate

Cam Houses

CAM FELL

Cam End

89

At Ten End, as the long descent to Hawes begins, the forward views improve quite dramatically, for ahead now lies Wensleydale and the grey buildings of Gayle and Hawes. Due north lies Great Shunner Fell, the next major feature along the Way, and to its right the Buttertubs Pass and Lovely Seat perched above it. Beyond that, the Pennine Way passes into Swaledale, bound for the northern edges of the Yorkshire Dales National Park.

From Ten End, where the track is forsaken for a cairned and grassy path going right, the way down to Hawes is obvious, descending Rottenstone Hill and past Gaudy House to reach Gaudy Lane, a walled track which goes down to meet a lane. Turn right, then left across fields, heading for Gayle, a small village on the edge of Hawes once famed for the quality of its residents' knitting.

The Way comes down to a flight of stone steps and along a lane then down a track to meet a road. Go right then left through a squeeze stile to pursue a slabbed path through a housing estate, a modern component of Gayle. After this the Way goes left along a road, then right, on a path above Gayle Beck, finally taking the path to the right of the church to emerge on to the main street in Hawes.

Hawes, granted a market charter in 1700, is a friendly, welcoming town, a bustling and delightful mix of narrow alleyways and attractive cottages, concealed nooks and crannies, and, it seems, a comely and haphazard indifference to planning law so that the whole ambience of the town hints at great antiquity. Yet in this respect at least, Hawes is a sham. When the Domesday surveyors passed this way, Hawes was no more than forest land, and later looked upon

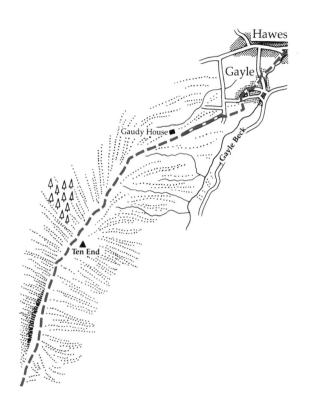

by Camden as "a dreary waste and horrid silent wilderness among the mountains...In this part goats, deer, and stags of extraordinary size find a secure retreat". Today, Hawes is the capital of Wensleydale, famed for its eponymous cheeses. Before departing, however, it is worth remembering that the next sizeable place along the Pennine Way is Middleton-in-Teesdale, so the town provides the last chance to stock up on essential supplies (including cheese).

Hawes to Keld

12 miles (20km)

The immediate prospect on leaving Hawes is a brief walk by road and across meadows to Hardraw where, at the rear of the Green Dragon Inn, lies the great natural bowl that receives the waters flowing over Hardraw Force, England's highest waterfall. To view it, however, a toll must be paid at the inn. Beyond Hardraw, a long haul leads across Great Shunner Fell and down into upper Swaledale at Thwaite, soon joining the Swale as far as Keld, where it meets the Northern Coast to Coast Walk, pioneered by Alfred Wainwright. The whole of the walk to Keld is both interesting and beautiful, and a delight. Even the most dank of days has to try hard to penetrate the pleasure of the long, striding walk down to Thwaite and the equally agreeable saunter through Swaledale to Keld.

Take the side road just to the west of the car park at the eastern end of the town, crossing a bridge over the disused railway line, then leaving the road at a gate to cut a corner into an area known as Haylands. This meadowland diversion soon leads back to the road and across the River Ure at Haylands Bridge. A woefully brief association with the River Ure ends at a path, signposted to Hardraw, that runs across more meadows to the village made famous by its impressive waterfall.

Entrance to see the falls is through the Green Dragon Inn for a nominal fee. It is unquestionably worthwhile doing so, and will scarcely lengthen the day, while offering an elaborate excuse for a drink at the inn for those thirsting after the effort of the 1¼ miles (2km) slog from Hawes! The vertical fall of the water is about 100 feet (30m), spewing clear of the Yoredale series cliff face in a most dramatic fashion.

The Way moves westward out of Hardraw, crosses a bridge spanning the erstwhile Force waters, and turns right along an enclosed drove road. It soon reaches open fell country, rising through terrain reminiscent of the Peak and the Cheviot to come. The route climbs steadily, with the beauty of Cotterdale to the left, and the valley of Hearne Beck rising to Fossdale Moss on the right. As the Way ascends, it forks right at Hearne Top, keeping to the main line of ascent as it veers to a more northerly direction. In so doing, Fossdale Moss and Lovely Seat assume more prominence as views to the west become obscured.

In spite of numerous false summits, steady plodding soon brings the top of Great Shunner Fell underfoot. With only a stone shelter, rebuilt in 1996, to protect against inclement weather, there is nothing other than a complete circle of outstanding views to delay the long sweeping descent to Thwaite. It begins by crossing a fence, moving north-east to Beacon Cairn, then arcing around the catchment area of Thwaite Beck to reach a walled track leading down to meet the road into Thwaite a little north-west of the village. On entering the village the route passes a former chapel, now converted into flats, then the Kearton Restaurant.

The restaurant commemorates Richard and Cherry Kearton, who lived in Thwaite before moving to London.

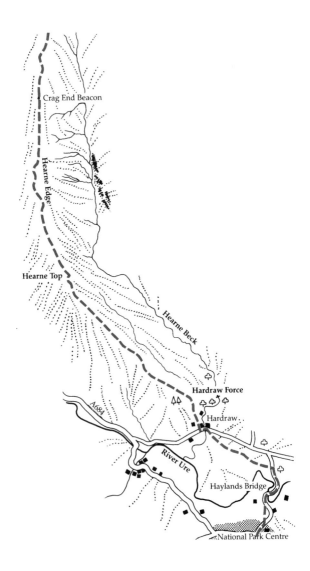

Crag End Beacon

Hearne Edge

Hearne Top

Hearne Beck

Hardraw Force

Hardraw

A684

River Ure

Haylands Bridge

National Park Centre

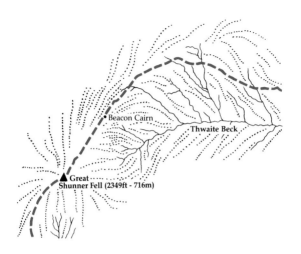

*Both were famed naturalists and wildlife photographers.
The village is a charming arrange-ment of old stone
cottages huddled together as if protecting one another
from winter storms. A look back from a short distance
further on along the Way shows that Thwaite, whose
name signifies that it was a clearing in a forest, lies snugly
tucked in a fold of Great Shunner Fell.*

The Way takes to a side street, then by walled path
and stiles to cross pastureland across the lower
slopes of Kisdon Hill. Beyond the low meadows,
the path rises through the intake, or inbye, fields,
gradually working a way round into the wide
trench that holds the River Swale. Without losing
height significantly, the route heads northwards
along the steep flank of Kisdon Hill, then north-
west across stony ground and through woodland
to meet, south-east of Keld, the Northern Coast to

Coast Walk. Both routes combine as they cross the river near East Gill Force and Kisdon Force (both worthy of attention), but their association is short-lived as they hasten on their separate ways.

Walkers bound for Keld should do so before crossing the river. It lies just a short distance by track and lane on from the river crossing.

Keld is attractively situated, the first and last village in Swaledale, and completely hemmed in by high moors. It is an ancient settlement of Scandinavian origin, its name meaning a place by the river. Once remote, Keld has benefited from the attentions of Pennine Wayfarers and Coast to Coast walkers. A youth hostel does good trade during the summer months, as do the various cottages and farms that offer bed and breakfast, and there is a small campsite. Even so, overnight accommodation is limited, so pre-booking is a good idea in view of the significance of Keld as a cross-over point on Britain's two most popular long distance trails.

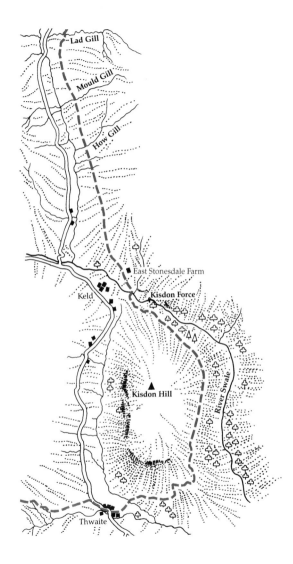

Lad Gill

Mould Gill

How Gill

East Stonesdale Farm

Keld

Kisdon Force

Kisdon Hill

River Swale

Thwaite

Keld to Tan Hill

3½ miles (6km)

Beyond the River Swale, the Way begins to leave behind the characteristic Dales scenery of farm meadows, river valleys and barns, and climbs into the embrace of the North Pennines. A first taste of this sterner country is included in this section on the final walk up to Tan Hill, the highest pub in England. Here the Way leaves the national park, heading for a National Nature Reserve and an Area of Outstanding Natural Beauty.

Across the River Swale, the Way goes left up a short, steep track to East Stonesdale Farm. It then continues by a grassy drove road, leaving the walls behind as the ascent eases along the rough eastern flank of Stonesdale, almost parallel with the minor road that ascends on the opposite side of the valley. Beyond Frith Lodge the terrain becomes increasingly bleak and barren, no longer archetypal Dales country, but a taste of North Pennine landscapes to come.

As Lad Gill is crossed, the Way, here a rutted track, changes direction, heading now north-east across Stonesdale Moor as a cairned trail, known to have been used by miners and possibly during Roman times, that crosses a particularly wild and desolate stretch of moorland, pock-marked by the scars of lead and coal mining.

Packhorse trails crossed these moors from a number of directions, converging on the Tan Hill Inn, which now lies only a short distance ahead.

Tan Hill Inn and the roads that converge upon it are a legacy of the coal mining industry that took place high on these moors as long ago as the 13th century. The inn is an 18th-century building, formerly known as King's Pit House, and in spite of the modern road having removed some of its loneliness, it remains a very isolated place.

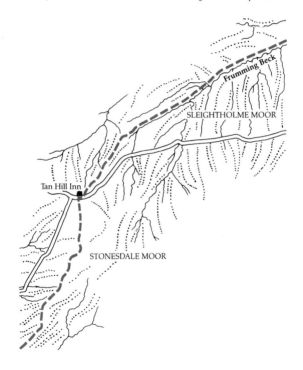

4 The North Pennines

Beyond Tan Hill Inn, the Pennine Way leads onward into the northern Pennines, where, as Alan Hall explains in his thorough and well-researched book, North Pennines, *the "endless fells and probing dales present a divergence of geological architecture, embroidered by the visible evidence of man's presence and passage through the centuries". The region is also laced with traces of man's administrative meddling: once the Pennine Way passed through Durham, Westmor-land and Cumberland, historically rich and much-loved old counties. Now only the first survives, while the latter two have joined forces to become the sprawling county of Cumbria.*

The North Pennines form a massive expanse of heather and tussock-grassed moorland, a comparatively little-known area within which lies the largest concentration of English hills outside the Lake District. It is also an important part of our national heritage, a fact underlined by the designation of a sizeable chunk of it as an Area of Outstanding Natural Beauty.

There is much remote country here; exciting, challenging and invigorating. It will thrill many, intimidate a few, but provide many jotous memories.

Tan Hill to Middleton-in-Teesdale

16 miles (25.5km)

Between Tan Hill and Middleton-in-Teesdale, the Pennine Way takes a route across low, open moors and through the valleys of Lunedale and Baldersdale before descending into Teesdale. There is a strong feeling of isolation on many stretches, and the onset of poor weather can make the passage a trying one. At other times, the breezy, heathery moorlands give enormous pleasure and excitement, further enlivened by the attractions of the Baldersdale reservoirs and those on the approach to Teesdale. Walkers wanting a shorter day can head along an official alternative to Bowes, though the direct route via God's Bridge is more scenic. Both routes join in Baldersdale.

From Tan Hill the Way heads north-east across Sleightholme Moor, along a barren, peaty, cairned route with little shelter. It keeps to the north bank of Frumming Beck, crossing numerous feeder streams and on to Sleightholme Moor Road. In poor visibility, it is better to follow the road north-east from Tan Hill, later branching left along Sleightholme Moor Road to rejoin the main route as it nears Sleightholme Beck.

Beyond this junction, the Way is seldom far from the beck, and runs on down past Sleightholme Farm set in a green hollow. Soon after, leave the now-metalled road at a gate and head down to cross Sleightholme Beck at Intake Bridge.

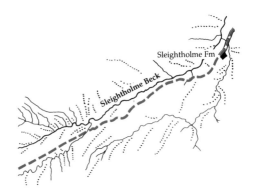

Over the bridge, walk parallel to Sleightholme Beck as far as Trough Heads, where the Bowes variant branches right (see below).

From Trough Heads Farm, go left, across heathery moorland to a wall, and then on to meet the River Greta at God's Bridge, where the river disappears beneath great slabs of limestone, which for a short while has replaced the gritstone outcrops of the moors. A lime kiln stands nearby. Pass the kiln and keep on past a farmhouse and a disused railway to reach the A66.

Crossing the busy A66, now that it has been dualled, is virtually impossible to accomplish safely. As a result the Way uses a diversion to a tunnel a short way up the road, and then heads on to the heathery expanse of Ravock Moor in a generally north-westerly direction, rising steadily. Ravock Castle is not as imposing as its name might suggest,

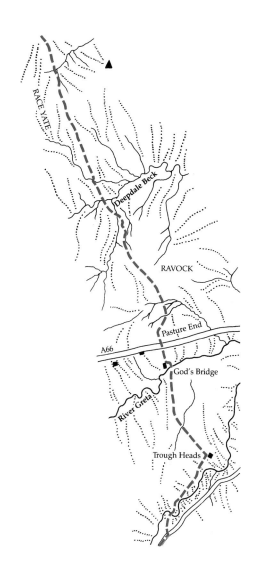

RACE YATE

Deepdale Beck

RAVOCK

Pasture End

A66

God's Bridge

River Greta

Trough Heads

in fact it is no more than a collapsed stone hut. Once around Ravock, the Way descends to the streams of upper Deepdale, here called Sleddale, crossing by a footbridge before pressing on by a wall to Race Yate Rigg, where the wall is abandoned and the route continues across Cotherstone Moor, with the reservoirs of Baldersdale beckoning ahead. Along the way, the alternative loop from Bowes rejoins the main route.

As the route across Cotherstone Moor reaches a surfaced lane, follow this for a short distance to Clove Lodge, beyond which the route descends across pastureland to Blackton Bridge, overshadowed by the huge dam of Balderhead Reservoir.

Tan Hill to Middleton-in-Teesdale via the Bowes loop. 20 miles (32km)

(Those not taking in the loop go to page 106)

The Bowes Loop is soon likely to be officially dropped because of the impassability of the route between Lady Myres Farm and Swinholme at times when the River Greta is swollen. The route is given here for those who need to head for Bowes, but the possibility of difficulties following bad weather should be borne in mind.

The loop to reach Bowes starts by branching right at Trough Heads Farm and continuing to meet an access track from West Mellwaters Farm, following this to East Mellwaters Farm (campsite). From here, the Way follows a wall and then heads left, across pastures to the River Greta, and then soon recrosses

Sleightholme Beck as it presses on to Lady Myres Farm. From the farm take a lane that leads out to a road into Gilmonby, a small village south of Bowes.

The village occupies a strategic position along the Stainmore Gap, where the Romans built a fort, Lavatrae, to defend their road from Penrith to Scotch Corner. Little remains of the Roman fort since Bowes Castle was built over it, and though this, too, is in a ruinous state, it still occupies a prominent position above the village.

St Giles Church, Bowes, is late medieval with Norman doorways, and in its graveyard in 1838, Charles Dickens stumbled on the burial place of George Ashton Taylor, a young boy whom he used to create the character Smike in Nicholas Nickleby. *Dickens also modelled Dotheboys Hall on the Bowes Academy at the west end of the village. The Academy was run by William Shaw, a man who had often been fined for maltreating pupils, and who, in the hands of Dickens, became Wackford Squeers, one of a breed of evil men he described as "traders in the avarice, indifference, or imbecility of parents...to whom few considerate persons would have entrusted the board and lodging of a horse or a dog".*

After leaving Bowes, the Way uses a lane to reach and cross the A66, pressing on through an area of moorland where Ministry of Defence warning signs recall the evils of war. The route bears left across Tute Hill, although the lane serves just as well to reach the track heading for Levy Pool. Cross Deepdale Beck, and head roughly northward, on to moors that are largely trackless and still bear testimony, in the shape of numerous abandoned dwellings, of difficult times past, when families struggled to eke out a living from the harsh landscape. Beyond an expanse of marshy ground around Hazelgill Beck, the Way crosses Kearton Rigg to traverse below the welcome gritstone landmark of Goldsborough, a comforting reassurance that the walker is still on the correct line. The route soon reaches an unenclosed lane.

Take this lane, left, and press on to rejoin the main line near Clove Lodge (the easier option), or leave it after a few strides to go north to East Friar House Farm, heading west from there across fields to reach Blackton Bridge.

End of Bowes loop section

With both routes now joined, cross Blackton Bridge, beyond which the Way swings out to pass close by Birk Hat Farm, made famous by TV tales about Hannah Hauxwell who lived here, and now part of a nature reserve. After Birk Hat, the route continues more or less northward on a gravel path through meadows, passing High Birk Hat Farm to reach a minor lane that leads, right, to Hury.

Turn left at the road, and then right, on to Hazelgarth Rigg, following a wall for a short time, before descending into Lunedale, where there are two massive reservoirs, Selset to the west and Grassholme. On reaching a lane near How Farm, go right to a junction, and then left to descend on a lane that crosses Grassholme Reservoir. Climb beyond to Grassholme Farm, go through the farmyard, and then head uphill through more pastures that in spring are vivid with wild flowers.

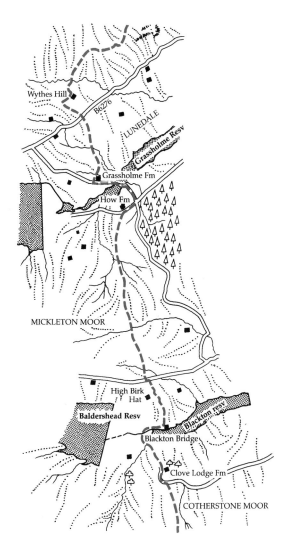

Wythes Hill

B6276

LUNEDALE

Grassholme Resv

Grassholme Fm

How Fm

MICKLETON MOOR

High Birk
Hat

Baldershead Resv

Blackton resv

Blackton Bridge

Clove Lodge Fm

COTHERSTONE MOOR

107

Cross a road and follow a track towards Wythes Hill Farm, heading left from there, and gradually bearing north-east around Harter Fell and into the patchwork fields of Teesdale that make a vivid and exhilarating impression when first glimpsed from the slopes of the fell. The Way, well-waymarked throughout, descends through lush pastures to a gate, from which it drops to a road just after a disused railway. The road (B6277) leads on to cross the River Tees and rise into Middleton-in-Teesdale, though the Pennine Way leaves the road before reaching the Tees.

Middleton-in-Teesdale is a small town of dour, yet attractive, cottages and buildings, that largely developed in the 1800s under the paternalistic influence of the Quaker-run London Lead Company, for whom Middleton was its northern administrative centre. The town grew from an Anglo-Saxon farming community, and much of the surrounding countryside still holds evidence of these early days.

Middleton-in-Teesdale to Dufton

17 miles (28km)

Some of the most beautiful country passed through by the Pennine Way lies between Middleton and Dufton. But it is also the wildest and loneliest section across shaggy moorland. The stretch begins in company with the River Tees, which, especially in its upper reaches, is one of the most attractive rivers in Britain, becoming increasingly boisterous the further north you go.

Near the great Cow Green reservoir, the Way traverses to the village of Dufton on the far side of the Pennine watershed, a frustrating and illogical deviation perhaps, since at the end of the day Wayfarers end up further from their ultimate destination than when they began. But the reasoning behind this imaginative digression becomes evident once the stunning threshold of High Cup Nick is reached, for this is simply too good to miss. Couple this with the opportunity (one that also makes good walking sense), of visiting the highest summit of the Pennines before pressing on to the North Pennine villages of Garrigill and Alston and the Scottish border, and the trans-Pennine loop becomes well justified.

Wayfarers setting off from Middleton can anticipate a change from moorland meanderings. The Tees (its name is said to mean a surging river), is fairly quiet and orderly around Middleton, but it later lives up to its name providing some of the most outstanding river scenery in the country. Often the already peaty brown waters are churned furiously into amber, cream-topped foam that

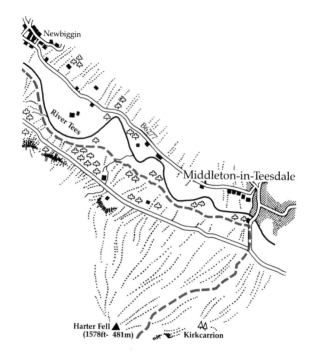

harmonises splendidly with the surrounding landscape.

From Middleton, the Way resumes along the south bank of the River Tees by a track that leaves the road just south of the Tees bridge. Initially, the Way maintains a fairly straight course, ignoring the Tees' sensuous meanders, but as it passes Park End Wood and reaches Rowton Beck, it descends to keep the river company. Eventually, the Way reaches Wynch Bridge, a suspension bridge that allows visitors to Bowlees along the B6277 to approach the Tees where it is at its most thunderous and extravagant best.

The original Wynch Bridge was built for miners in 1704, but it was rebuilt in 1830 after a collapse ten years before. A short way on from Wynch Bridge, and well seen from it, the Way reaches Low Force, a spot where the riverbed is wide and punctuated with islands of dolerite set against an enchanting background of woodland.

Continuing beside the Tees, the route travels easily on towards the distant rumbling of High Force, the most famous of Pennine waterfalls.

Juniper bushes proliferate along the Way, especially here and above Keedholm Scar. Now more usually found in garden centres, juniper was formerly gathered to produce high quality charcoal, and its berries used to flavour gin,

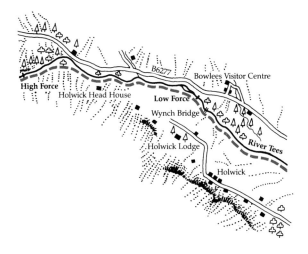

a word that derives from genévrier, the French for juniper.

Only as the Way bends sharply just after Keedholm Scar does the sound of High Force really begin to intrude. Soon it comes into view framed by trees, a dramatic plunge over a lip of dolerite and shale, falling 70 feet (21m), into a spray of fine mist.

The Way presses on above High Force, where the noise suddenly decreases as the energetic river, born of the high mountains ahead, flows less restlessly. By comparison with High Force, the double falls of Bleabeck Force are nothing, and soon passed as the route crosses brackenless Bracken Rigg before turning north, bound for Cronkley Farm. From the farm, press on northward to its access bridge, and cross the river.

Walkers may wish to halt here, either in Forest-in-Teesdale or a little way north-west at Langdon Beck village, where there is a youth hostel and an inn.

From Cronkley Bridge, the Way runs along the north bank of the Tees to Sayer Hill Bridge, which leads across Langdon Beck. Follow a track to Saur Hill Farm (Sayer Hill), going left in front of the farm and across pastures, with the crags of Cronkley Scar rising across the river to the south-west. The route returns to the river for a short while before diverting away to pass around Widdy Bank Farm, then returning to the river.

It curves with the river, passing beneath the rocky whinstone ramparts of Falcon Clints, cliffs that are populated by the smaller birds of prey, and where

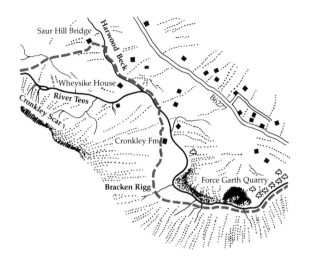

the harshness of the rock is brightened by green ferns and lichens.

Keeping close to the scree and bouldery base of Falcon Clints, the Way arrives at the confluence of the River Tees and Maize Beck. It is the latter that will generally guide the route onwards across the lonely moors that lie ahead, but for the moment, the Way is forced spectacularly up beside the foaming torrent of Cauldron Snout, a most memorable experience.

Here the now-dammed waters of the Tees released from the embrace of Cow Green Reservoir, frolic and foam in their new-found freedom, plunging relentlessly through a narrow break in the Whin Sill, an intrusive, igneous rock. It is the product of that blazing, volcanic interlude in the geological timescale that took place millions of years ago. As the rocks cooled, so they formed quartz-dolerite, appearing here in Teesdale, and later at High Cup Nick and Northumberland, as the Whin Sill.

During spring this area is enlivened by the outstanding array of wild flowers for which Teesdale is renowned, not least the remarkable spring gentian, at home in the Alps and the Pyrenees, and here alongside such other delights as alpine forget-me-not, bitter milkwort and bog sandwort. The whole area is now embraced within the Upper Teesdale National Nature Reserve, and the region's rarities are protected by a knowledgeable ranger. Carbon

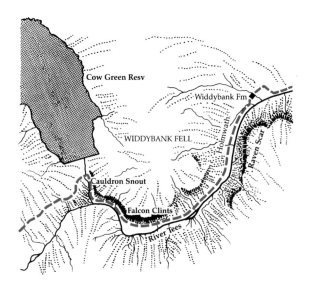

dating clearly shows that some of the pollen found in the peat dates from the end of the last Ice Age, protected on grassy islands in a sea of forest, fragments of the tundra conditions which covered Britain at that time.

Plans to dam the lazily flowing Tees and flood the valley to form Cow Green Reservoir in the 1960s led to a deluge of complaints and a public inquiry. The inquiry rejected the appeals from botanists, and the valley was flooded in 1971-72, but not before many of the rare plants had been relocated above the proposed water line. The reservoir now disputes with Chew Reservoir, on the northern edge of the Dark Peak, the distinction of being the highest reservoir in England. When the reservoir is full it possesses a splendidly wild and natural air about it, but if the water is low the imprint of man's interference rings the water's edge, a sad and unsightly memorial.

A little modest scrambling is needed to reach the top of the Cauldron Snout rocks, across which great care is needed. A left turn leads across the Tees to gain a surfaced track heading south-westwards to Birkdale Farm.

Go through the farmyard, beyond which the surfaced track becomes grassy, soon descending to cross Grain Beck, and on, guided by a tall cairn on the fellside above, to Moss Shop, once basic bunkhouse accommodation for the miners who worked in this area. From here, the route heads roughly westward across largely featureless terrain that used to be confusing in misty conditions, but across which the Way is now either flagged or surfaced.

The vast area to the north is broadly known as Dufton

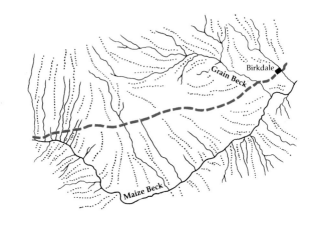

Fell, an enormous silent, sombre and sodden wilderness some of which has been given the name Meldon Hill. To the south-east and south-west lie Mickle Fell and Murton Fell, which are a military training area in which walkers are not generally encouraged, as numerous warning signs on the maps suggest.

The Way keeps well to the north of Maize Beck for a while before rejoining and crossing it to continue towards High Cup Nick along its south bank. If flood conditions prevail and the beck cannot be forded, an escape route, keeping to the north side of Maize Beck, is available, and leads to a footbridge, from where the route continues to reach High Cup Nick.

Heading south-west, the route crosses High Cup Plain towards the deep chasm of High Cup Nick.

This is a spectacular moment, all the better for the suddenness with which it appears from this direction. At High Cup Nick where High Cup Gill falls across a lip of dolerite into an enormous ice-carved coomb, a great montage of green river valley, silvered stream, scree and towering grey/brown whinstone cliffs opens out ahead.

Westward in clear weather the distant peaks of Lakeland are especially notable. The path, keeping the chasm well to the left, continues south-west below the flanks of Narrowgate Beacon, passing a prominent finger of fragile rock known as Nichol's Chair, standing in isolation amid a landscape of

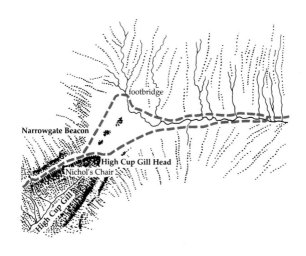

shattered pinnacles and crumbling columns of basalt.

Nichol's Chair, a precarious stack of basalt, is named after a cobbler who lived in Dufton, and who is reputed to have cobbled a pair of boots on the top of it.

As the valley widens, the Way rounds Peeping Hill and gradually descends to meet a well-defined track, once a drove road, that leads down through walled fields to the Vale of Eden, past Bow Hall and into Dufton at Town Head. Turn right into the village, though the official line of the Way goes round the back of the village, to the east and north of it.

Dufton is an alluring village built mostly of red sandstone set against the background of conical Dufton Pike. This is pure Westmorland; solid, squat, sandstone houses standing proud against the elements in a former lead mining area. It is an oasis below the heights from which the notorious Helm Wind blows. The Helm Wind is a remarkably ferocious and gusting wind caused by the air rising from the east and over the summit of Cross Fell, where it forms the helm or cap, and is cooled. It then rushes forcibly down the western side of the mountain,

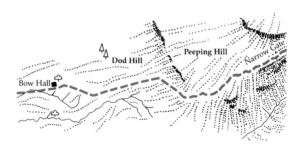

and has allegedly blown carts and farm vehicles over. Thomas Wilkinson of Yanwath, a friend of Wordsworth, wrote of the Helm Wind in his Tour to the British Mountains *(1824) how "if I advanced it was with my head inclined to the ground, and at a slow pace; if I retreated and leaned against it with all my might, I could hardly keep erect; if I did not resist it, I was blown over".*

Dufton to Alston

19 miles (30km)

The walk to Alston begins with a stiff ascent to Knock Fell, then follows good paths across the high grassy summits of mast-crowned Great Dun Fell, bald Little Dun Fell and stony Cross Fell to descend to the village of Garrigill. Riverside paths then lead on from Garrigill to Alston. This is not a section for the faint-hearted. It is a long and demanding day, but one that is undoubtedly rewarding. Nevertheless, the weather across the tops can be evil, and the effort of getting to the highest point of the Pennines the price that has to be paid for that long diversion to Dufton. A really adverse weather forecast might suggest an extra day resting in Dufton.

The Way continues from the northern end of Dufton village, setting off along a signposted lane to Coatsike Farm, dominated by the shapely cone of Dufton Pike. Beyond Coatsike, the route follows Hurning Lane, an ancient sunken way leading to deserted Halsteads. A short way on beyond Halsteads, the Way bends to round Cosca Hill, a minor extension of Dufton Pike, and then descends a little to cross Great Rundale Beck by an attractive clapper bridge.

Follow the line of a stone wall to a gate, and eventually on to a track slanting across the fellside towards Swindale Beck and Knock Ore Gill. Cross Swindale Beck on a footbridge to tackle a steeper ascent north-east along a path that leads, with beautiful retrospective views across the Vale of

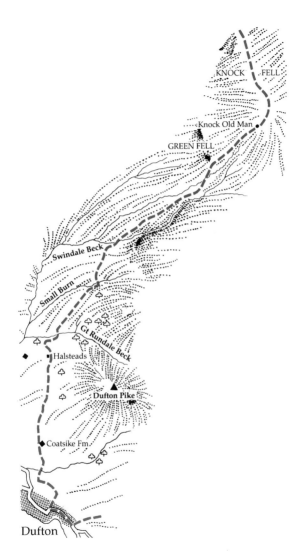

KNOCK FELL

Knock Old Man

GREEN FELL

Swindale Beck

Small Burn

Gt Rundale Beck

Halsteads

Dufton Pike

Coatsike Fm.

Dufton

Eden, along 'hush' sides directly to Knock Old Man, a fine squarish cairn. A short way on the summit of Knock Fell is reached, marked by a less imposing cairn, set against the humpy background of Great Dun Fell and Cross Fell.

Along the upper section above Swindale Beck a number of 'hushes' are encountered. These are man-made water channels, artificially created by releasing water dammed higher on the fellside, and used to scour away soil and vegetation from the underlying minerals, in this case lead.

On the face of it, there is little to linger over on Knock Fell, so the Way pushes on to and across the col with Great Dun Fell, and then on over Little Dun Fell, before reaching Tees Head and the final haul across stony ground to the plateau-like summit of Cross Fell. On closer inspection, however, there are some outstanding exposures of Carboniferous swamp forest fossils to be found, the highest in the Pennines.

Just before Great Dun Fell, Dunfell Hush can trap the unwary if it is still holding snow, which is often deep. Aim for the left (west) end of the hush, or simply use the access road to the radar station, though there is no right of way along it.

Along with its near neighbours, Little Dun Fell and Cross Fell, Great Dun Fell forms the highest ground in the Pennines. The presence of a radar station on its summit has made Great Dun Fell one of the most unattractive, if most useful, mountain tops in Britain. It lies at the heart of the ancient Milburn Forest, and appears as a flattened mound, its white geodesic dome teed up as if at the start

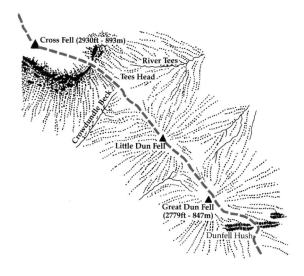

of a leviathan game of golf. The summits also lie along the watershed of Britain – rain falling on the west finds its way into the Eden and the Irish Sea, while on the east everything flows into the South Tyne or the Tees, bound ultimately for the North Sea.

The flagged continuation from Great Dun Fell to Little Dun Fell could not be simpler. Descend from the northern perimeter fence of the radar station to a boggy col beyond which an easy pull places you beside the cairn on the top of Little Dun Fell. The summit is uninspiring, and suffers from the proximity of its two higher siblings.

The next col, north-westward, is also flagged, and forms the birthplace of the River Tees, marking the boundary between the former counties of Cumberland and West-

morland. A short ascent leads through the ring of Cross Fell's ice-shattered screes and on to the summit plateau, across which an easy stroll on stony ground leads to the summit shelter and cairn, at 2,930 feet (893 metres) the highest point of the Pennine Way.

In fine weather, Cross Fell looks a calm, inviting place, a high whaleback that commands the most superlative views across the Vale of Eden to Lakeland. But its repertoire of dirty tricks includes sub-zero temperatures, rain, and snow well into the summer months. With the Helm Wind also to contend with, it is small wonder that the fell's original name was Fiends' Fell, before St Augustine (St Paulinus is also credited with the deed) erected a cross on the summit and built an altar to celebrate the Holy Eucharist in the hope of scattering the resident demons. Camden thought the building of crosses in prominent places such as the summit of Cross Fell was "an extraordinary piece of devotion... as being both nearer to Heaven and more conspicuous". If any demons dared to remain in the face of such devotion, the likelihood is that they finally vanished when some 50 brass bands assembled on the top of the fell to celebrate the passing of the Reform Act of 1832.

Daniel Defoe described the Pennines as lying "like a wall of brass" along the eastern edge of Westmorland. He was not far from the truth for they formed the mainstay of a sizeable lead mining industry, largely driven and inspired by the London Lead Company. Appearances are deceptive, and though Cross Fell looks solid enough (and no doubt is), it is honeycombed by shafts and levels that produced over three million tons of lead during the 18th and 19th centuries. Silver was also refined from the lead, and from 1725 to 1870 almost 5.5 million ounces were produced.

From the summit of Cross Fell, the Way sets off north-north-west through the ring of screes to reach a well-established track.

The track is said to be an old corpse road linking Kirkland and Garrigill, and one 18th-century funeral party, caught by a blizzard while undertaking the crossing, abandoned the deceased and hastened back to Garrigill, returning two weeks later when it was safe to do so. The coffin was taken back to Garrigill where it was buried in glebe land, subsequently consecrated by the Bishop of Durham, and so obviating the need for the corpse road.

The Pennine Way makes use of the corpse road down to Garrigill. Shortly after meeting the track, the Way reaches Greg's Hut, an emergency overnight bothy, and then heads down through the litter

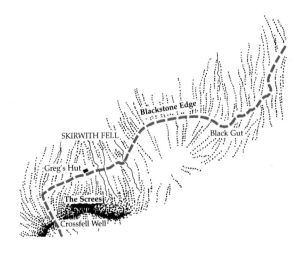

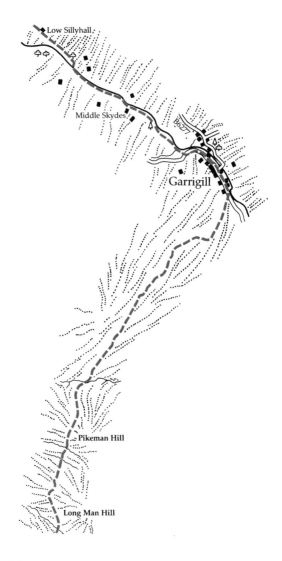

Low Sillyhall

Middle Skydes

B6277

Garrigill

Pikeman Hill

Long Man Hill

and debris of old mine workings that can yield small fragments of fluorspar and galena (lead ore).

Keeping left of Long Man Hill and Pikeman Hill, the Way heads northward for a while, and later north-eastward as it descends on to Black Band Moor. Finally, it reaches the valley road a short distance south of Garrigill. Turn left to the village.

Garrigill, charmingly set around a village green, is a quiet, secluded hamlet along the River South Tyne, and well off the tourist route. The village's name probably derives from Gerrard's Gill or Valley, and with it comes the first real "north-east" feeling, brought by the influence of the South Tyne.

The Way continues through the village, but when the road heads left, uphill, take a stile on the right to run parallel with the stripling South Tyne. Further on, a footbridge leads across the river near Low Sillyhall Farm, gradually moving away from the South Tyne as the route heads northward to Bleagate Farm and along well-established tracks through pastures and a well-defined walled track into Alston.

Alston is a delightful market town of steep, cobbled streets, venerable houses, shops and churches, lying close to the confluence of the South Tyne and the Nent. It is reputably the highest market town in England, lying at an altitude of around 300 metres. (Buxton shares the claim, and stands at about the same height.)

Although the town has a history going back at least to the 12th century when it was part of a royal estate used by the kings of Scotland, most of modern-day Alston is a product of the 19th-century lead mining industry that flourished in the region.

From the Way, which passes to one side of the town, the image is one of grey stone buildings among which whitewashed houses stand out, rising to a fine square-towered, steepled church. Historian William Hutchinson disparagingly described Alston as "meanly built, situated in a declivity of a steep hill, inhabited by miners. Pent in a narrow valley over which mountains frowned with a melancholy sterility and nakedness".

Alston to Greenhead

16 miles (26km)

Between Alston and Hadrian's Wall at Greenhead, the Way is not at its exciting best in spite of the splendid company of the River South Tyne for some of the distance. At other times, meadows and farms combine to complicate or confound route-finding, and demand concentration. As the end of this stretch draws near, however, the crags of the Whin Sill that bear Hadrian's Wall are a constant focus of attention, and a welcome sight.

The Way continues from the southern end of Alston, heading north on the west bank of the South Tyne. To reach it, cross the road bridge, and soon turn right on to the Slaggyford road (A689), from where the riverside continuation, which begins as a track, is signposted. At Harbut Lodge, the route is diverted westward to the A689, turning right along the road for a short distance before heading left across a field.

From a wall and stile, the Way performs a curious loop down a drove road that leads to Gilderdale Burn, before courting the burn for a while. No one uses this loop, and the official line is at the time of writing in the course of diversion: there is an old green road from GR703474 to GR698478, that is preferred, and in any case makes more sense. The Way soon changes course again, and sweeps around to reach the remains of Whitley Castle.

Whitley Castle is a Roman fort that defended the Maiden

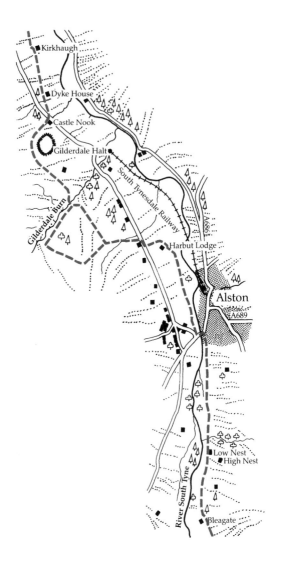

Kirkhaugh

Dyke House

Castle Nook

Gilderdale Halt

Gilderdale Burn

South Tynesdale Railway

A686

Harbut Lodge

Alston

A689

Low Nest

High Nest

River South Tyne

Bleagate

Way, a main supply route between the fort near the junction with the Stanegate (Carvoran) and Kirkby Thore. Its grassy ramparts and ring ditches are well-preserved, and worth exploration.

Beyond Whitley Castle the Way continues to meet the A689 again, crosses it, and presses on in a direction west of north and, from Kirkhaugh, north-west to Lintley Farm. From the farm it goes under a railway viaduct that now carries the South Tyne Trail, and then follows Thornhope Burn and later the South Tyne once more.

The A689 is met again at Thompson's Well Bridge, where it is followed into the quiet village of Slaggyford, which is grouped comfortably around its wide green on the grassy flanks of Williamston Common. By the time Thompson's Well Bridge is reached, the South Tyne is wide and shallow, and provides delightful riparian scenery. Sadly, from the bridge, the Way moves further and further away from the river, and never makes a close acquaintance with it again.

Leaving Slaggyford by a track beside a chapel the Way follows the line of the Maiden Way, much as it did for a short distance before the village. For a while paralleling the old railway line, the Way finally crosses beneath it, pressing on along a track across fields to Merry Knowe Farm. Then it continues across more pastures to Burnstones Farm, and out on to the open moorland of Glendue Fell. The directness of the route across the moor and the steady tread of booted feet may well call to mind the Roman soldiers of Agricola's army who

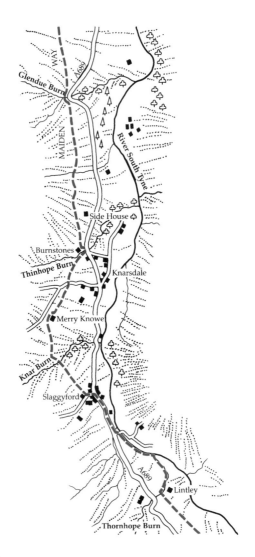

Glendue Burn

WAY

A689

MAIDEN

River South Tyne

Side House

Burnstones

Thinhope Burn

Knarsdale

Merry Knowe

Knar Burn

Slaggyford

A689

Lintley

Thornhope Burn

132

marched this way, far from the sun of home and no doubt quite miserable, in the 2nd century AD.

The route strays little on to the moorland, preferring to edge above the South Tyne valley and to flirt briefly once more with the A689 at the crossing of attractive Glendue Burn. The moor either side of the burn is largely trackless, so close attention to direction is important for a while. Beyond Glendue Burn lies Lambley Common, a managed, heather grouse moor and one across which the evocative call of the golden plover is often heard. Before the A689 is reached again near Lambley village the route veers to the left, but here the attraction of the moors gives way to an area scarred by mine workings.

High House is a ruined barn, and beyond it the Way crosses Hartley Burn and keeps on over farmland pastures, past Batey Shield Farm and Kellah Burn to a minor road. Turn up the track leading to Greenriggs, keeping to the left (west) of the cottage.

Continuing up a field and then roughly north-west, the Way is now bound for Round Hill, Glencune Burn and the wide, rolling expanses of Hartleyburn Common and Blenkinsopp Common. Passing close by the trig pillar on Blade Hill, the Way drops to Gap Shields, there turning right along a track through an unsightly area of disused mine shafts. The route now descends to the busy A69, meeting it half a mile (1km) west of Greenhead.

The quickest way into Greenhead is simply to turn

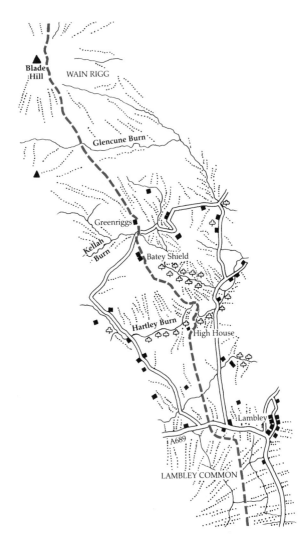

Blade Hill

WAIN RIGG

Glencune Burn

Greenriggs

Kellah Burn

Batey Shield

Hartley Burn

High House

Lambley

A689

LAMBLEY COMMON

right along the A69, but this is dangerous with passing traffic. The route across the road, climbing steep banks on the opposite side and then across fields and a golf course to reach the vallum, is to be preferred, although it adds a little distance.

The Vallum is a wide ditch that parallels Hadrian's Wall throughout its length, and this should now be followed east to the B6318, a short distance north of Greenhead, with a far safer walk into the village.

The church in Greenhead is relatively modern, designed by John Dobson, a famous Newcastle architect in the 19th century. Whether it contains any stones from the nearby Wall is uncertain, but many of the surrounding buildings do. Fourteenth-century Blenkinsopp Castle, south of the village, certainly does, and when the ruins of the castle were built into a farmhouse in 1880, numerous Roman inscriptions were found.

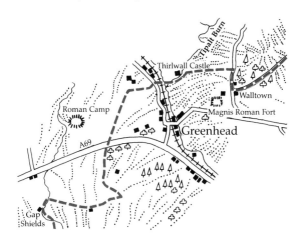

The fort of Carvoran, which the Romans knew as Magna, lies a little to the north-east of Greenhead. During Hadrian's reign it was garrisoned by a Syrian cohort of archers. In 1797, Sir Walter Scott was moved by the scenery around nearby Thirlwall to write his verses: To a Lady, with Flowers from a Roman Wall. In the same year he married Charlotte Carpenter, whom he had first met at Wardraw House.

It is at Greenhead, as much for convenience as for any other reason, that this section on the North Pennines comes to a close. Beyond now lies the massive Hadrian's Wall, Wark Forest and the Cheviot Hills, and if you could see for 90 miles, you could say the end was in sight.

5 The Cheviot Hills

At Greenhead the Pennine Way makes its first significant contact with Hadrian's Wall. Through-out the Pennines and along the route of the Pennine Way, evidence of the Roman occupation is encountered constantly, usually in the form of mine workings, camps or forts. Yet nowhere on this route is the profile of their presence so markedly apparent as along the Wall, constructed following the visit of the Emperor Hadrian to Britain in AD122. The only surviving comment on the reason for its construction is that it was to separate the Romans from the barbarians.

When the Wall was completed, it stretched from Wallsend-on-Tyne in the east to Bowness-on-Solway, a distance of 73 miles (117km), or 80 Roman miles. It was probably 15 feet (5m) high, with a parapet built above that. Along the Wall some 17 forts were constructed, the best surviving example at Housesteads. Between the forts at intervals of every Roman mile a small fort, or milecastle, was built, which could accommodate about 50 men. Between each milecastle were two turrets, which were used as signalling towers.

In front of the Wall a ditch was dug to increase the scaleable height, except where this was not needed, as along the Whin Sill crags. To the south of the wall another ditch, called the vallum, was constructed, marking the boundary of the military zone occupied by the wall and its armies. Its purpose was demarcation rather than defence.

From Greenhead the Way follows the Wall as far as Rapishaw Gap, a mile (1.6km) short of Housesteads, to which a visit is always worthwhile. Walkers intending to continue to Bellingham should take into account the extra time and effort even this modest extension might make to a long day. Once the Wall is left behind, the Way presses on through the Border forests, travelling forest trails and low moorland expanses before heading into the village of Bellingham. Beyond that the route hastens on to engage the Cheviot Hills, finishing the journey with the longest day of all.

The Cheviot Hills offer some of the most outstanding walking country in Britain, far above the forest tracts, where hilltop after hilltop roll onward through a landscape steeped in a troubled history. The hills themselves owe their origin to volcanic events 380 million years ago, when magma was forced up through Silurian strata. They were inhabited by Neolithic man and the Beaker people, by the Romans, who constructed their camp at Chew Green, and later by Norse invaders. From the 13th century, starting with an attack on the Scots by Edward I until long after the Union of the Crowns in 1603, they were the battleground of the

Border Troubles, a 300-year war of attrition between the English and Scots, English and English, and Scots versus Scots. The reiving forays between feuding families took little account of the Border, but every advantage of the terrain and the difficulties of government that it brought.

Greenhead to Bellingham

21 miles (33.5 km)

The Way leaves Greenhead northbound on the B6318, Gilsland road, soon leaving it at a gate to access a track past a row of red-brick houses and across a railway line. It presses on around a field margin, following Tipalt Burn to reach Thirlwall Castle.

The remains of Thirlwall Castle, a fortified tower built in the 14th century with stones from Hadrian's Wall, stand perched on a small hillock. It is thought that Edward I rested here on 20 September 1306, on his final journey north to vanquish the Scots: the king died less than a year later at an encampment on the banks of the Solway Firth.

Go right, in front of the castle, and descend to cross the Tipalt Burn by a footbridge, continuing on a walled track into woodland before heading eastwards along the line of a ditch that once formed part of the defences on the northern side of the Wall. As the crest of a hill is reached, so the Way enters the Northumberland National Park, its third and final National Park. Moving eastwards, the Way arrives at the site of the Agricolan fort of Carvoran, beyond which the view of Walltown Quarry is not the most attractive of sights along the Way, though landscaping by the National Park Authority has done much to improve its appearance.

A stony road continues the eastwards thrust of the route, passing the quarry, and moving on until it becomes possible to head uphill to reach the Wall

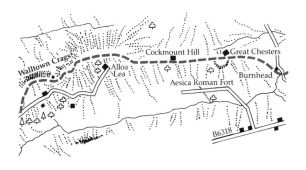

itself close to Turret 45a. The Wall will be the route's companion for some time now, although it is far less imposing than it would have been when first built. The official Way actually takes the line of the military supply road, but most Wayfarers prefer to keep close to the course of the Wall.

In 1995, an announcement was made that a new National Trail was to be developed along the length of Hadrian's Wall, now a World Heritage Site. This will take at least until the year 2001 to come to fruition, and until then will simply not exist. Walkers inspired by this brief acquaintance to tackle the entire Wall walk, will have to be patient, and should avoid any attempt to do the walk before it is complete. Visitors walking along the top of the Wall have caused considerable damage, including the partial collapse of the Wall in places. Under no circumstances should Pennine Wayfarers walk on top of the Wall; please keep to the adjacent path and set an example to others.

Trekking along the line of the Wall is an inspirational and atmospheric experience, and one to be savoured. The view northwards to the darkness of Wark Forest, Kielder Forest, and the bleak lands of the "barbarians", does much to enhance the frontier aspect of the Wall as it was during the time of its occupation.

The Way now pursues the Wall eastwards passing the remains, in various stages of preservation, of turrets and milecastles. Less noticeable are the remains of Great Chesters, a fort known as Aesica, which was constructed some time after the building of the Wall.

Beyond Great Chesters the Way descends and, guided by a drystone wall, reaches Cawfields Quarry, now a National Park picnic site set beside a large quarry lake. Keep on past the quarry to gain Cawfield Crags and one of the best sections of the Wall, before reaching Windshield Crags and then the Steel Rigg car park.

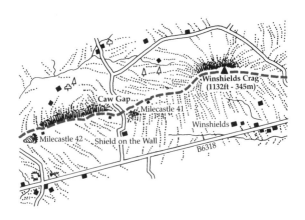

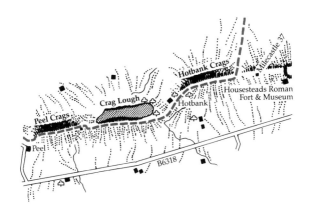

Either side of Steel Rigg it is easy, and tempting, to walk along the top of the Wall. But it should be resisted in the interests of preserving this amazing survival of Roman Britain. Beyond Steel Rigg the Wall undulates dramatically along the crest of the Whin Sill crags. Highshield Crags, a short way ahead, are especially stunning, set directly above the blueness of Crag Lough. After passing the lake, the Way crosses Hotbank Crags and descends to a natural cleft in the Whin Sill at Rapishaw Gap. Here the Way takes its leave of the Wall.

Walkers wanting to visit the fort at Housesteads, and with both the time and energy to spare, should continue along the line of the Wall, subsequently retracing their steps to Rapishaw Gap. From Rapishaw Gap the Way heads out across moorland to the west of Broomlee Lough, a favoured haunt of over-wintering wildfowl.

Once the route moves away from the Wall there is a

dramatic change of scenery as it enters a wilderness area where dark Whin Sill escarpments rise above tall, golden grasslands. Bathed in sunlight this is one of the most impressive sights in Northumberland, but in poor weather its greyness sends walkers scurrying for the cover of the forest.

Before long the route begins its first skirmish with the Forest of Wark, entering it by a broad track. Rising gradually, the Way follows the track and then branches right on a grassy ride that leads out of the forest. Another stretch of moorland ensues before re-entering the forest at a standing stone known as Comyn's (Kimmins) Cross. More forest rides lead on to reach a lane near Willowbog Farm. There the Way turns right along the lane for a short distance, before leaving it near Ladyhill for another grassy forest track heading north.

The passage through the forest is short-lived and soon emerges on to Broadpool Common, the way across indicated by a signpost on leaving the forest. Before long the route courts a stream, and passes a small cascade to reach Fawlee Syke to the north of Ground Rigg. Once beyond the syke and over Longlee Rigg the green beauty of Warks Burn comes into view, to which the Way descends, crossing it by a footbridge.

Beyond Warks Burn farmland predominates, and the route presses on to Horneystead (B&B), near the remains of an early 17th-century pele tower, then reaching a minor road near The Ash Farm. The Way continues past Leadgate Farm and past low crags to reach Lowstead Farm, an attractive arrangement of

buildings built largely around a former 16th-century bastlehouse, a fortified farmhouse.

Linacres Farm, by contrast, is a modern building beside which the Way turns east along a surfaced lane to a junction, and then north-north-east to a T-junction. Continuing as a field path, the route keeps on to descend towards Houxty Burn, a delightful tree-lined stream.

Across the burn, the route keeps on past another farm, grandly-styled Shitlington Hall, and then goes uphill to reach the sandstone outcrop of Shitlington Crag. The heathery moorland of Ealingham Rigg lies to the north-west, and rolling pastures and dark forests beyond.

A few moments here is well worthwhile, to survey the extremely pleasant pastureland through which the Way has just passed, a rich mosaic of farm fields and buildings and dark green forest swathes.

The route reaches a wall not far from a radio relay station. Go east along a track, and then turn sharply north-east across damp moorland to touch on a minor lane before descending to reach the B6320 north-west of Bridgeford Gate Cottage. The road is now followed for 2 miles (3km) – the longest road section on the route – to Bellingham, crossing the River North Tyne by a three-arched bridge built in 1835 by John Green of Newcastle, and turning right at a T-junction to enter the town.

Bellingham, pronounced Bellin-jam, is a lively market town that Wayfarers should take advantage of before

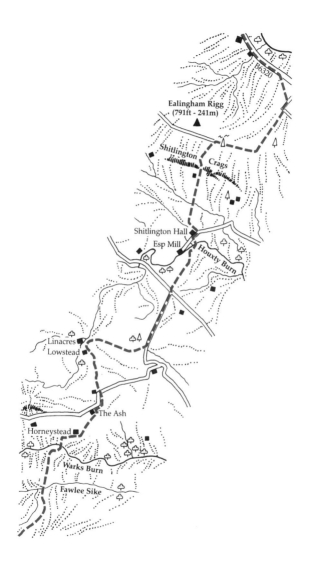

heading off on the final stages to Kirk Yetholm. The North Tyne is especially beautiful here, and the town does it justice. For centuries, Bellingham's survival rested on the whims of the predatory Redesdale reivers for whom this community on the very limits of England was an easy target. It was to protect against their tendency to fire all in their wake that the church of St Cuthbert, twice destroyed in this way, was reconstructed around 1200 with a stone roof.

Bellingham to Byrness

14 miles (23km)

From Bellingham the Way heads across more pastures and across the heather moorland of Padon Hill to reach the depths of Redesdale Forest and the isolated community of Byrness, set on the road to Carter Bar.

From Bellingham the Way takes the West Woodburn road, descending to cross Hareshaw Burn, and along a lane that climbs past the youth hostel. Leave this at a sharp right-hand bend, and head roughly north on a farm access leading to Blakelaw Farm, going through the farmyard. The route continues across hillside pastures, heading for a small group of pine trees on the skyline. Nearby, the Way passes through a gate and out on to moorland once more to reach the boundary of the Northumberland National Park where an alternative to the official line of the Way offers itself.

The main line heads for Hareshaw House Farm, keeping to the higher ground. (A lower alternative, branching left at the National Park boundary and following the line of a fence, is intended to avoid disturbance to stock at the farm, but is not endorsed by the Pennine Way Co-ordination Project.) A wide access track runs on from the farm, a relic of a small mineral railway that closed in the 1950s, and eventually follows another track to reach the B6320 Bellingham-Otterburn road.

Across the road a track rises to the wide, heathery

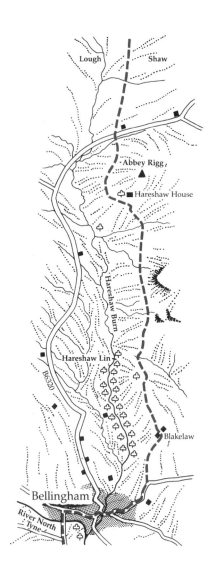

Lough Shaw

Abbey Rigg

Hareshaw House

Hareshaw Burn

Hareshaw Lin

B6320

Blakelaw

Bellingham

River North Tyne

hillside of Lough Shaw which on a clear day offers a stunning panorama. Across Lough Shaw the Way heads for Whitley Pike, heading west-north-west then north beside a fence. From the top of Whitley Pike, the route (again with a slightly shortcut

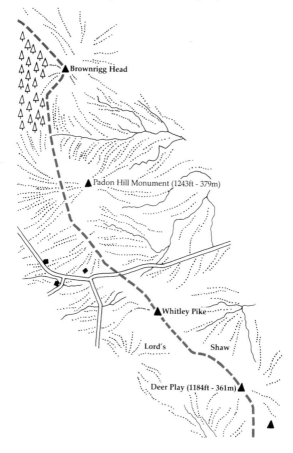

version) heads for an unenclosed road, beyond which it rises in company with a fenceline on to Padon Hill, crowned by a massive bee-hive monument constructed in the 1920s by the former owners of Otterburn Hall.

Padon Hill is said to be named after Alexander Peden, a Scottish Nonconformist minister who held services on the hill during the reign of Charles II, when Nonconformist religious gatherings were being repressed.

The Way descends beside a fence and through great swathes of heather towards the boggy col linking with Brownrigg Head, from there climbing beside Gib Sheil Plantation to reach the highest ground. Now the Way has forest on the left and open moorland to the right as it moves along the boundary of the former estate of Gabriel Hall, High Sheriff of Northumberland in the early 19th century. Small boundary stones inscribed with the letters GH mark the limit of his estate.

The great blanket of the Redesdale Forest is entered at Rookengate (GR799956), from where a forest trail heads west of north, and allows speedier progress. There are a few breaks through the trees to raise hopes that civilisation is still out there, somewhere, but generally the scenery is one of trees and more trees. Eventually, the route descends to Blakehope-burnhaugh Farm.

The farm arguably holds the record for the longest name in England, though Cottonshopeburnfoot to the north-west has recently laid siege to the claim by combining Cottonshope and Burnfoot to give an even longer name.

Cottonshopeburnfoot

Blakehopeburnhaugh

Hindhope Burn

Wind Burn

Between these two long-named settlements, the Way follows the east bank of the River Rede, then crosses to the west bank and along a forest trail until it descends to cross the river again. It finally rises to the terraced 1930s' Forestry Commission houses of Byrness, on the A68 Newcastle-Jedbergh road, the last chance for replenishments before the vast wilderness of the Cheviot Hills.

Byrness was originally built to accommodate the 1,000-strong workforce engaged for 15 years on building the Catcleugh Reservoir. Later it housed employees of the Forestry Commission carrying out the planting of Redesdale Forest. A youth hostel, hotel, B&B and farm accommodation encourage many Wayfarers to halt here.

Byrness is on the A68, a busy thoroughfare that meets the Anglo-Scottish border at Carter Bar. In winter the road often becomes blocked with snow, and was formerly used by the Chevy Chase, the famous Newcastle-Edinburgh coach which tackled the ascent until the mid-1840s when the Anglo-Scottish rail link was completed at Berwick.

Byrness to Kirk Yetholm

25 miles (40km): 27 miles (44km) if The Cheviot is included

This final leg is by far the longest day on the whole route and is difficult to shorten by anyone not carrying their overnight lodgings on their back. If the whole section cannot be completed in one go, the only alternative is to descend from the main route at Chew Green, Beefstand Hill, north of Mozie Law, or Clennell Street (north of Windy Gyle). These arrangements require good planning, pre-booking of accommodation, and a precise idea of how much extra walking is involved.

From Byrness a surfaced lane leaves the road 50yds/m north-west of the Byrness Hotel, former home of Jacob Robson, Master or Joint Master of the Border Hunt for more than 50 years. Follow the lane as far as Byrness Cottage, where it becomes possible to re-enter the forest. Unrelentingly steep slopes on grassy rides through flanking conifers, bracken bands and outcropping crags, finally leave the forest just below the top of Byrness Hill, which is ringed by outcrops.

Forest cloaks the hillsides to the west, while to the east the land drops to Cottonshope Burn, part of the vast Ministry of Defence estates in this part of Northumberland, based on the military camp at Otterburn. The Ministry of Defence owns almost a fifth of the total area of the Northumberland National Park.

A narrow path through grass leads northwards to

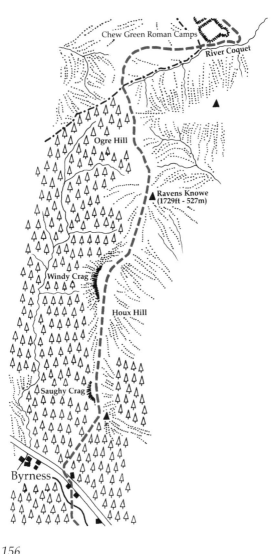

Chew Green Roman Camps

River Coquet

Ogre Hill

Ravens Knowe
(1729ft - 527m)

Windy Crag

Houx Hill

Saughy Crag

Byrness

Houx Hill, from there following a fenceline to Ravens Knowe and Ogre Hill, beyond which lies the Border, at the northern tip of the Redesdale Forest. A stile over the Border fence takes the Way into Scotland for the first time, evincing feelings that the end is in sight.

J.H.B. Peel describes these final stages as "a moor as wild and lonely as any in England. No trees are here; neither shrub nor scrub nor reed; only the music which we call silence, and a peace so profound that, when you lie on the grass, its vibration soothes your civilized fever".

In Scotland, the route continues northwards beside a fence, before turning east and descending to the Roman encampment at Chew Green, low grassy earthworks that once were home to Roman legionaries. The Way, now back in England, passes around the encampment, heads north and briefly steps back into Scotland before continuing above the heads of Long Sike and Buckham's Walls Burn.

The Way now arcs eastwards, and sets off on a generally north-eastwards course. A fence accompanies the route as far as Auchope Cairn, with the worst stretches along the way having now been paved. South-east of Lamb Hill a wooden hut serves as an emergency refuge for anyone caught by a sudden change in the weather.

Lamb Hill leads on to Beefstand Hill and Mozie Law, just east of which the long-established cross-Border drove road known as The Street is met, linking Calroust and Upper Coquetdale. Beyond The Street, the Way continues easily up to Windy

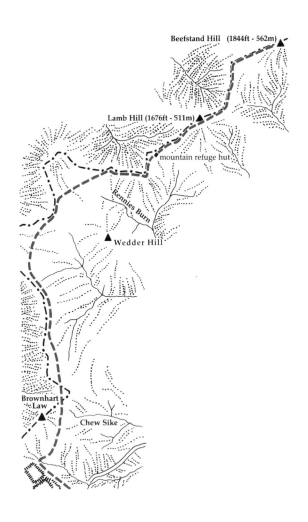

Gyle, marked by an enormous spread of stones, often mistakenly called Russell's Cairn, which stands a little way further along the route, north of the Border fence.

In 1585 Sir Thomas Kerr of Ferniehurst and Sir John Forster of England assembled with their supporters at a Warden's Court high on the Border ridge to deal with complaints. Lord Francis Russell, son-in-law of Forster, was also present in spite of being the object of a grudge nursed by Kerr. During the Court a disturbance broke out among bystanders which Russell attempted to quell. For his trouble he received a bullet in the chest from which he died. Kerr was subsequently relieved of his warden-ship, though whether the shooting was accidental or premeditated is not clear. In commemoration some of Russell's soldiers are said to have built a large cairn at the spot where the incident took place, hence Russell's Cairn.

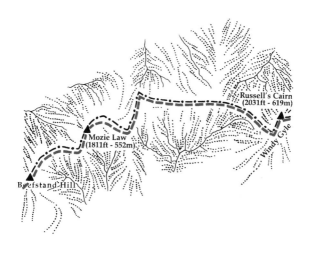

The supposition has long been that the pile of stones on the top of Windy Gyle marks the place where Russell died, but this is probably a pre-historic burial mound.

From Windy Gyle, the Way continues along the border fence to the Border Gate, where another ancient highway, Clennell Street, crosses the ridge. The Pennine Way presses on following the Border over King's Seat to the Hanging Stone, a low outcrop of rocks that marked the boundary between

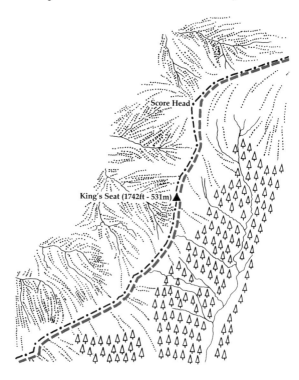

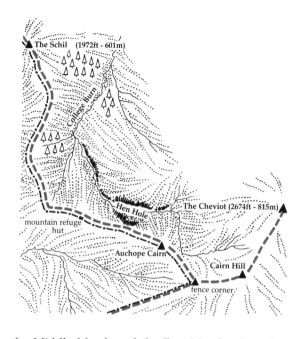

the Middle March and the East March when the Border was managed by marcher lords.

The task of a marcher lord was often a luckless one. A memorandum of 1579 suggested that the decay of the English Marches was due to raids by the Scots, neglect of horses and arms, castles and forts being in unworthy hands, and deadly private feuds between many of the families, made worse by intermarriage.

A short way on, the Border fence turns sharply left, and here a decision must be taken whether to extend the walk to visit the top of The Cheviot.

Paving now makes the journey much easier than it once was, but if it comes late in a long day, with some distance yet to go, anyone feeling weary should decide to make the acquaintance of The Cheviot on another day.

Follow the fence, left, over Auchope Cairn, from the top of which there are good views down into the College Valley, and ahead to the next summit, The Schil, one of the finest in the Cheviot Hills.

The summit of The Schil is ringed by a surprising outcrop of rocks and boulders, part of a metamorphic aureole of "baked" andesite that once circled the high ground that is now The Cheviot. Directly above the head of the College Valley, on the col before The Schil, a refuge hut will be found useful by anyone caught in worsening weather. It stands just above a landslip known as Red Cribs, mentioned as long ago as 1597 when it was described as "a passage and hyeway for the theefe".

Beyond The Schil the Way sticks with the Border fence for a while longer before branching into Scotland, dividing there for the final stage just east of The Curr. The original line returns to the Border fence at Steerrig Knowe and follows this north for a quite steep ascent over White Law. Here it dog-legs before continuing north, over lands inhabited since prehistoric times, to cross the Border again on Stob Rig. Beyond it continues on a good track, keeping to the south of Green Humbleton, which is crowned by the spectacular earthworks of an Iron Age hill fort, and descending to cross Halter Burn.

The second possibility, rather kinder to weary legs,

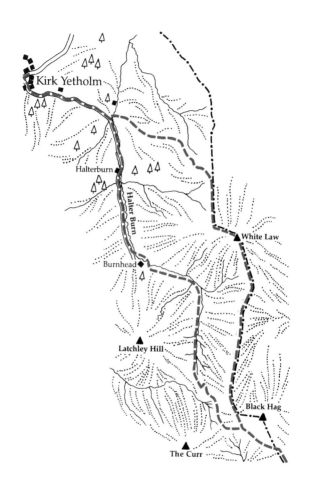

follows a bad weather alternative that descends to
the head of Halter Burn, circles round Burnhead
Farm, and then joins a surfaced lane that leads out of

the valley. The two routes combine just after the original line crosses Halter Burn. Channelled into an enclosed lane at a cattle grid, the Way begins its final steps. A short road walk and the final ascent of the whole journey is all that remains, crossing the northern shoulder of Staerough Hill to descend to journey's end at Kirk Yetholm. A Pennine Way marker near the Border Hotel is generally considered to be the official finishing point, though many feel the bar of the Border Hotel serves just as well.

Kirk Yetholm was once a Romany stronghold. The last Romany queen, Esther Faa Blyth died in 1835 and was buried here. The gypsies were far from popular, and even ordered to leave the kingdom by Elizabeth I, on pain of death, a prospect they chose to disregard. The final impressions of the Pennine Way will not rest on the trials, tribulations and many pleasures that will have gone before. In time, when the miscellany of aches and pains has gone, the true magnitude of what has been achieved will sink in, and all those experiences, good and bad, will come flooding back to be relived time and time again.

Tackling something as demanding as the Pennine Way, whether it is in parts or as one complete journey is no mean feat. But often the end of the journey is an anticlimax, as one's sense of purpose evaporates. Suddenly, the incentive that has driven the walker on for day after day no longer has anything to do. It takes time to adjust, and time to reflect. Only then will you fully begin to realise what you got out of it.

Meanwhile, many congratulations!

North to South

Kirk Yetholm to Byrness

25 miles (40km): 27 miles (44km) if The Cheviot is included

The southbound Pennine Way begins along a lane opposite the Border Inn, climbs across the shoulder of Staerough Hill and descends to a cattle grid near Halter Burn. A choice of routes is now available. By turning right along a lane, the Way accompanies Halter Burn, eventually rising as a path to join the main line at a col between The Curr and Black Hill.

The main line crosses Halter Burn at a ford and then pursues a rising track across the southern edge of Green Humbleton to reach the Border, following this and climbing south. Near White Law, the route dog-legs to White Law summit, then resumes a generally southerly direction to meet the lower, alternative route near Black Hill. From the col, the Way rises to cross The Schil and continues across a shallow col above Red Cribs to rise over Auchope Cairn to a sharp right turn. At this point, Wayfarers must decide whether to visit The Cheviot. If the intention is to continue all the way to Byrness, to include The Cheviot involves additional walking in what is an already long first day.

From the right turn, descend via Hanging Stone and Kings Seat, and then pursue the border fence over a succession of summits beginning with Windy Gyle. Mozie Law, Beefstand Hill, Lamb Hill,

Blackhall Hill and Brownhart Law follow before reaching the Roman camp at Chew Green.

At Chew Green the Way swings west to Coquet Head, then south over Ogre Hill, Ravens Knowe and Houx Hill to reach Byrness Hill directly above a steep descent to the village of Byrness.

Byrness to Bellingham

14 miles (23km)

From Byrness, the Way starts opposite the inn, and goes behind the little church before it drops to meet and cross the River Rede, then follows its banks as far as Cottonshopeburnfoot, where it crosses to the opposite bank to reach Blakehopeburnhaugh. Travelling roughly east of south, the Way continues from Blakehopeburnhaugh into the depths of Redesdale Forest, leaving the forest at Rookengate. It then heads south-east from Brownrigg Head and south over Padon Hill, before pressing on to Whitley Pike.

Leaving Whitley Pike the Way heads south-east and then south over Lough Shaw to reach the B6320 Bellingham-Otterburn road. Cross this and keep on past Hareshaw House, where a low level alternative to the path that passes close by the House leads to the Northumberland National Park boundary. Continuing southwards, the route reaches Blakelaw Farm and then swings down to rejoin the B6320 on the outskirts of Bellingham. Follow the road into the town.

Bellingham to Greenhead

21 miles (33.5km)

The Way leaves Bellingham heading west to cross the North Tyne bridge, then follows the B6320 across the North Tyne Bridge until, near Bridgeford Gate Cottage, it rises, right, across fields to touch on a minor lane for a short distance, before following a track that leads south-west then north of west to a relay station. A short way on the route swings roughly southwards past Shitlington Crags and on to Shitlington Hall Farm. A little distance further the Way crosses Houxty Burn then climbs south-east over pastures to follow the line of an old hedge to a T-junction of roads. Cross to and follow the road directly ahead, but leave it after a short distance to head for Lowstead Farm.

A succession of delightful farms; Leadgate, The Ash and Horneystead leads the Way onward. Then it crosses Wark Burn and rises over moorland to enter a forest through which a trail leads to a road near Ladyhill Farm. Turn right at the road until, south of Willowbog Farm, the Way turns south once more, enters forest for a short while, and leaves at Comyn's Cross. A brief stretch of moorland, heading south-west, leads back into forest, there swinging south and eventually leaving the forest not far from Broomlee Lough.

The Way keeps to the west of Broomlee Lough and continues to meet Hadrian's Wall at Rapishaw Gap. The Roman fort of Housesteads involves a diversion eastwards but it is well worth a visit.

The route now follows Hadrian's Wall westwards over Hotbank Crags, Highshield Crags and Peel Crags to the Steel Rigg car park, then continues over Windshields Crags to Caw Gap. Keep on westwards over Cawfield Crags, passing the remains of Great Chesters fort, to reach Walltown Crags. Then the route moves south-west to pass through an area of quarries before finally heading for the outskirts of Greenhead, near the ruins of Thirlwall Castle. A short distance down the B6318 leads into Greenhead, though the Pennine Way actually continues westwards along the line of the vallum before swinging south-west to meet the busy A69.

Greenhead to Alston

16 miles (26km)

The Way continues from the A69, west of Greenhead, leaving the busy road at GR651652, along a track that leads into an area of disused mine workings, swinging west along a track to reach Gap Shields Farm. The route then continues south and south-east across the moorland of Blenkinsopp Common, heading for Round Hill and the farm fields around Greenriggs, just beyond which it crosses Kellah Burn. It continues to Batey Shield Farm, crossing a minor road on the way, and then veers south-east to cross Hartley Burn.

High House, a short way on, is a ruined barn beyond which the Way continues in a generally east of south direction as it approaches Lambley village, to the west of which it crosses the A689. After crossing the A689 near Lambley, the path swings left before pressing on beside a fence along the flanks of heathered Lambley Common, along the line of the Maiden Way. With the River South Tyne now a companion in the valley below, the Way dips to cross Glendue Burn. It returns to moorland crossing the side of Proudy Hill to reach Burnstones Farm.

Still high above the valley, the route briefly touches upon the A689 again, then passes through pastures to reach Merry Knowe Farm, before changing direction to reach Slaggyford. Beyond, it follows the A689 for a little way before descending to the River South Tyne. Visiting Lintley, Kirkhaugh and Dyke House, the Way is never far from the river until it veers away to reach Whitley Castle, a Roman fort.

Beyond the castle, more pastureland leads on to reach Gilderdale Burn, before the Way recrosses the A689, and follows a track to Harbut Lodge, beyond which the route reaches Alston near the bridge spanning the South Tyne. The village lies across the bridge, close to the confluence of the South Tyne and the Nent.

Alston to Dufton

19 miles (30km)

The Way continues south from Alston by returning to, but not crossing, the South Tyne bridge. It accompanies the river, at various distances, to Bleagate Farm and Low Sillyhall Farm before crossing the river by a footbridge. Keeping close to its banks, it reaches a minor road rising from Garrigill, which is followed to reach this splendidly isolated village.

A short distance south of Garrigill, the Pennine Way ascends Cross Fell, the highest of the Pennines. An enclosed track leads to Black Band Moor, though the official line takes a shortcut that few walkers bother with. Higher up, heading for an extensive area of former mining activity, the route crosses Pikeman Hill and Long Man Hill before changing its direction and heading for the watershed, west of north of the summit of Cross Fell. On the way it passes Greg's Hut, an emergency shelter.

The Way rises through Cross Fell's ring of screes to reach the summit plateau on which the shelter and cairn that marks the highest point stand forlorn amid an ocean of stones. Continuing now in a south-easterly direction, the route descends towards Tees Head and on across Little Dun Fell and Great Dun Fell. Over this section, the route has been paved, and the way forward is unmistakable.

Beyond the radar paraphernalia of Great Dun Fell, the Way descends around Dunfell Hush to the col below Knock Fell, then ascends to this stony fell top on which the massive cairn of Knock Old Man is a good marker. From the cairn a path descends south-westwards beside old hushes to cross Swindale Beck. Lower down the route crosses Great Rundale Beck and circumvents Cosca Hill before moving on to reach the deserted building at Halsteads. An ancient sunken way, Hurning Lane, now leads on to Coatsike Farm and down into

Dufton. The official line of the route passes behind the village on its north and east side to reach Town Head, though most walkers will enter the village for an overnight halt.

Dufton to Middleton-in-Teesdale

17 miles (28km)

From the southern edge of Dufton, the Way leaves the road at Town Head for an old drove road, that rises past Bow Hall and passes south of Dod Hill and Peeping Hill. Soon the first real impression comes of the chasm of High Cup Gill. The path moves closer to the valley, across which the immense walls of Whin Sill are outstanding. Further along, the Way passes beneath Narrowgate Beacon and presses on to reach High Cup Nick, where the waters of High Cup Gill spill over the edge of the cliffs.

The route now crosses High Cup Gill and heads eastwards to accompany Maize Beck, pursuing its southern banks, before fording it and continuing along its northern side. When Maize Beck swings south-east, the Way, largely flagged or stone surfaced, keeps to a more easterly and then north-easterly course, heading past Birkdale Farm and the outflow of Cow Green Reservoir. After crossing a bridge beneath the walls of Cow Green Dam, where the River Tees is met again, the Way swings south, scrambling down the slippery rocks to the base of Cauldron Snout, one of the most impressive waterfalls along the route. A short way on Maize Beck is met again at its confluence with the Tees.

Now the route follows the north bank of the Tees, below Falcon Clints and on to pass Widdy Bank Farm, before meeting Langdon Beck at Saur Hill Bridge. It then courts the river as far as the access track to Cronkley Farm, beyond which it rises past the farm and on to Bracken Rigg before resuming a more or less faithful riparian relationship.

High Force is passed en route, an impressive moment, with the Way then continuing past Keedholm Scar to Low Force and Wynch Bridge. The route stays close by the river as far as Park End Wood, when a more direct line to Middleton-in-Teesdale is preferred to the river's meandering. The Way meets the B6277 a short way south of Middleton, which is reached across the bridge.

Middleton-in-Teesdale to Tan Hill

16 miles (25.5km)

The Way continues south along the B6277 for a short distance to a gate near a bend in the road. Here it leaves the road, ascending across farm pastures to pass around Harter Fell before descending to Wythes Hill Farm and the B6276.

Cross the road and go down into Lunedale and Grassholme Farm, passing through the farmyard to reach a lane. Go left along the lane, which crosses Grassholme Reservoir, and rises to a T-junction. Go right, leaving the lane at How Farm, and climbing across the wedge of land between Lunedale and Baldersdale, to which the route eventually descends. Turn left on meeting the road to Hury, then right to reach High Birk Hat Farm and shortly, Birk Hat Farm, former home of Hannah Hauxwell.

The Way crosses Blackton Bridge, between Balderhead and Blackton reservoirs, and rises to Clove Lodge. At this point there is an option to take the Bowes Loop, for walkers intending to stay overnight in Bowes. This loop is likely to be dropped as an "official" line before long because of difficulties after heavy rain along the section between Swinholme and Lady Myres Farm. The description for the loop is given below.

Middleton-in-Teesdale to Tan Hill via the Bowes Loop

20 miles (32km)

After crossing Blackton Bridge, the easiest way to begin the loop is to keep on as far as the lane just after Clove Lodge and to follow this roughly eastwards until the Way leaves it north-west of Goldsborough Hill. The alternative is to follow a waymarked route through a succession of fields to East Friar House Farm, reaching the lane, southwards, from there. From the lane, the route moves south of gritstone Goldsborough Hill to reach How Beck Head, before swinging to a more southerly direction across Kearton Rigg and Hazel-gill Beck.

Now the route rises on to moors where abandoned farmsteads are a notable feature, descending to cross Deepdale Beck near Levy Pool Farm. A short distance on, the route meets the end of a track, but heads past West Stoney Keld Farm and Tute Hill, though the lane serves just as well, since the official line rejoins it after a short distance.

The lane is followed into Bowes, beyond which the Way heads for the village of Gilmonby, changing direction there and heading west to cross the River Greta near Swinholme. It is between here and Lady Myres Farm that passage can be frustrated. If this occurs, the only solution is to retrace your steps to Bowes and to follow the A66 to Pasture End, where the main route crosses. This is a dangerous undertaking since the dualled A66 carries high-speeding and heavily-laden traffic. A nearby tunnel makes life much safer. Beyond Lady Myres Farm the Way continues across fields to West Charity Farm, just beyond which it crosses Sleightholme Beck and follows a wall towards East Mellwaters Farm and then to West Mellwaters. Now the route veers southwards to reach Trough Heads Farm, there rejoining the main route.

From Clove Lodge the Way presses on to meet a lane for a short distance before rising on to bleak Cotherstone Moor. Beyond Race Yate Rigg, the route follows a wall as it descends into Deepdale, then, having crossed a stream by a footbridge, it rises again to reach the collapsed stone hut that bears the grand name of Ravock Castle. Across Ravock Moor, the route descends to meet the busy A66, which must be crossed carefully. Beyond the A66, the route descends to the natural limestone architecture of God's Bridge and the River Greta, then continuing south and south-east to Trough Heads, where the Bowes Loop rejoins the main route.

The Way continues along Sleightholme Beck, which it crosses at Intake Bridge, and rises to meet an access lane to Sleightholme Farm. The route follows Sleightholme Moor Road, which, if visibility is poor or the weather especially bad, should be followed to reach the lane that runs westwards to Tan Hill Inn. Otherwise, the route eventually leaves Sleightholme Moor road and keeps along the course of Frumming Beck finally to reach the Tan Hill Inn, where it enters the Yorkshire Dales National Park.

Tan Hill to Hawes

15¹/₂ miles (26km) (Keld: 3¹/₂ miles/6km)

The way to Keld from Tan Hill is all downhill. In poor conditions the lane can be followed, but the main route, a rutted track, heads southwards from the inn on to Stonesdale Moor. Once across Lad Gill, the Way follows the course of Startindale Gill as it parallels the road, passing Frith Lodge and eventually meeting the River Swale near East Stonesdale. Here the river is crossed, and the route briefly shared with the Northern Coast to Coast Walk. Across the bridge, Keld lies to the right (west), but the Way starts climbing around the flanks of Kisdon Hill, high above but following the course of the river, until the route swings to the south-west, descending through fields to reach Thwaite.

Leave Thwaite village by turning right, as if following the road to Keld, but leave this for a walled track that ascends on to the moors north of Thwaite Beck. This swings south-westwards to

Beacon Cairn and the final haul to the top of Great Shunner Fell. Beyond that, a long descent begins on a moorland ridge sandwiched between Cotterdale to the west and the valley of Hearne Beck, with Fossdale Moss rising beyond. Eventually, the descent is channelled into an enclosed drove road that leads down to the road at Hardraw.

At the road turn left towards the village and over a bridge. If time permits visit the spectacular falls of Hardraw Force, reached on payment via the Green Dragon Inn, which, after the crossing of Great Shunner Fell, may prove to be a good idea in more ways than one. Across the bridge, the Way heads south-east across fields to meet Brunt Acre Road, following this across the River Ure at Haylands Bridge and cutting a corner before rejoining the road for the final stage into Hawes.

Hawes to Horton-in-Ribblesdale

14 miles (22.5km)

The Way leaves Hawes by a path beside the church that leads to Gayle, continuing by a narrow path through a housing estate and across fields by a paved way to West End. At a stile, the Way enters a field where it keeps ahead for a short distance until it changes direction and heads for a lane. Turning right and left, the route leads along Gaudy Lane to Gaudy House. Just before reaching Gaudy House, branch left and begin the long, gradual ascent across the flanks of Dodd Fell Hill to reach Kidhow Gate, to meet the surfaced road linking Hawes and the isolated farmstead at Cam Houses (B&B). From

Kidhow Gate, the route follows a course south-west, along a Roman road (Cam High Road), which it shares with the Dales Way for a while. At Cam End the two trails part company, and the Pennine Way turns abruptly southwards, meandering downhill to reach Ling Gill Bridge.

Beyond Ling Gill an old packhorse trail is followed around Fair Bottom Hill and Cave Hill to Old Ing Farm. The Way continues to the southern edge of Greenfield Plantation, before turning south, through a gate and then by a well-defined track, later accompanied by a wall to Horton.

Horton-in-Ribblesdale to Malham

14 miles (22.5km)

The Way leaves Horton-in-Ribblesdale at the southern edge of the village, along a signposted and enclosed track that sets off north-east, apparently in completely the wrong direction. Finally, at a gate, it turns eastwards and begins the ascent of Penyghent on a resurfaced section, rising to the edge of the summit plateau, before changing course again and heading south as it climbs to the summit.

Cross a wall and turn right, following the path to the two-tiered prow of Penyghent, descending through rocks that can be slippery and awkward before reaching easier ground. The route now heads across moorland to Churn Milk Pot, and then heads for Dale Head Farm, using its access track out to the Stainforth-Halton road. Turn left along the road until, near a cattle grid, it is left to follow a wall that starts the ascent of Fountains Fell. The top of the rise crosses the fell a short distance north-east of the highest point, to which a diversion may be made. The whole area, however, is riddled with open mine shafts, and exploration is not advised in poor visibility.

Across the ridge, the route descends rapidly on an old mine track to meet the Stainforth-Arncliffe road via the access to Tennant Gill Farm. A brief ascent from the road leads through fields on a green path running roughly southwards to a gate. Go left, near a house, and on along a broad track that continues to reach Tarn House.

The route now passes round Malham Tarn, close to the woodland on the south-eastern shoreline, heading for a car park where the water from the tarn outflows beneath the road. Turn right along the road, cross a bridge, and then turn left, heading across level ground to a place where the water flowing from the tarn disappears from view at Water Sinks. Now follow a deepening dry valley, until it curves sharply to avoid Comb Scar, a dry waterfall. Here the route doubles about to reach a stile at the head of a tributary gully which gives easy access to the dry valley of Watlowes.

Follow this valley until it reaches the limestone pavement directly above the cliffs of Malham Cove. Branch right across the limestone pavement, taking special care if the rocks are wet, and continue to a stile at the head of a long flight of steps that descend to the base of the cove. A short deviation to visit the base of the cliffs is worthwhile. A clear path now heads out of the valley to a road gate, through which a left turn leads to Malham.

Malham to Thornton-in-Craven

10¹/₂ miles (17km)

The Way continues southwards from Malham on the east bank of a stream, following a surfaced path for a while before heading across fields to Hanlith, where it meets a lane. Along the way, the waters from Malham Tarn issue at Aire Head and from here onwards the accompanying watercourse is the infant River Aire. The route never strays far from the river as it heads southwards past Kirkby Malham and Airton to reach Newfield Bridge.

The Way crosses the bridge and continues with the river for a short distance recrossing it to touch briefly on a lane. The route now crosses the fields of Eshton Moor to reach the southern boundary of the Yorkshire Dales National Park at a hill crest wall. Now a waymarked route descends to a lane leading south-east into the village of Gargrave, which is set in a wedge of land between the River Aire and the Leeds and Liverpool Canal.

The route leaves Gargrave by a lane at the southern end of the village, over a bridge spanning the River Aire. Leave the lane, on the right, and cross fields to reach the Leeds-Kendal railway line. Beyond, a surfaced lane leads the Way onward to reach Scaleber Hill, over which there is an easy descent through more fields to a bridge adjacent to Trenet Laithe. After a short stretch along a lane, the Way cuts a corner (left), to rejoin the lane and head for Williamson Bridge and the Leeds and Liverpool Canal. The route follows the canal towpath as it passes beneath the busy A59 road. Before long the Way leaves the canal and climbs Langber Hill, then dropping to Langber Beck. The route continues across sloping fields towards Old Cote Farm, keeping to the right of the farm to reach a rutted track that leads to a row of terraced cottages and Cam Lane, a narrow surfaced lane. This leads south into Thornton-in-Craven.

Thornton-in-Craven to Cowling

6 miles (10km)

From Thornton, the Way descends lanes to pass beneath an old railway bridge, continuing to Brown House Farm. Pass through the farmyard, and climb through meadows to reach Clogger Lane. Turn right along the lane to a T-junction. Cross the road ahead and go past old quarries and up to Pinhaw Beacon, which offers a spectacular view of the surrounding countryside.

A sandy path continues through heather across Elslack Moor to Hewitts Farm, using the farm access road to reach White Hill Lane. Cross the lane and then follow good paths above Stansfield Beck through meadowland, to reach Lothersdale near the Hare and Hounds Inn.

Turn right into the village and keep ahead over a bridge, shortly leaving the road, left, to climb steeply beside a wall to reach Woodhead Farm, from there descending to reach Surgill Beck. The path rises through more fields to meet a lane at a sharp bend, and follows the lane to Over House Farm, where it turns right to follow the lane to Cowling Hill Lane. Turn right and then left on paths leading to the derelict High Stubbings Farm, then descending to reach Gill Bridge.

A short bout of road walking follows along Gill Lane, before the Way leaves the lane to pass Middleton and continue southwards to Ickornshaw and the A6068.

Cowling to Hebden Bridge

14¹/₂ miles (23.5km) (Ponden: 3¹/₂ miles/6km)

From the A6068 walled pastures lead to Lower Summer House, beyond which a green lane and more walled tracks head for the waterfall at Lumb Head. A number of ruined farmsteads are passed before the route reaches and crosses Andrew Gutter by a footbridge, rising steadily on a cairned path across bleak Ickornshaw Moor.

Gradually the Way rises to pass to the east of Wolf Stones Hill before heading south-east to Old Bess Hill, where a wall and fence guide the Way over Thornton Hill to reach Crag Top. Continue down to reach a lane, and turn left, following the lane for a short distance until it is abandoned, on the right, to descend through fields to reach the Colne-Haworth road near the western end of Ponden Reservoir.

Cross the road and go over a bridge at the head of

the reservoir, contouring above the reservoir on a track that goes past Ponden Hall. Follow the track around the reservoir to reach Rush Isles Farm. Turn right here, following a walled track, and climb by a long flight of steps to a row of cottages. Near the cottages, cross a step stile and turn left along a broad track leading to a minor back road at Buckley Green. Turn sharp right, past Buckley Green, and soon go left, beside a wall, ascending on to open moorland. After crossing with a dilapidated wall, the path enters an enclosed section ending at a stile.

Turn right after the stile, and follow a track that passes Upper Heights Farm and ascend to Top Withins, of Brontë fame. Keep on past Top Withins to cross the watershed between Round Hill and Dick Delf Hill, from there descend to meet the middle of the three Walshaw Dean Reservoirs. Turn left and follow the reservoir to the dam between the middle and lower reservoirs.

The official line crosses the dam at this point, swinging left to follow a surfaced reservoir road out to meet the Brierfield-Hebden Bridge road. [At the time of writing, there is a temporary diversion in operation at this point, taking the Way along the southern shore of the lower reservoir, crossing its dam, and resuming the route from there.]

Turn left along the Brierfield-Hebden Bridge road to a narrow path descending on the right to the confluence of Graining Water and Reaps Water, crossed by footbridges below Gorple Lower Reservoir dam. The Way continues up to Gorple Cottages, and heads south over the featureless landscape of Heptonstall Moor. But it soon changes direction and passes to the north of Standing Stone Hill, the highest point hereabouts, gradually swinging round to Clough Head Hill and down to Mount Pleasant Farm and Long High Top Farm.

After Long High Top Farm, the route heads for the hamlet of Colden, on the Blackshaw Head-Heptonstall road. The route descends to cross Colden Water, where both the Pennine Way and the Calderdale Way meet, and keeps south over Pry Hill to Badger Lane. More fields lead south to the steep ground overlooking Calderdale, through which the Way then threads a route to the ruins of a chapel, past cottages, and on beneath a railway bridge that once served the Lancashire and Yorkshire Railway. Finally, the route descends a side road known as Underbank Avenue to reach the A646, with Hebden Bridge two miles (3km) away to the left along the road. If Hebden Bridge is the objective, a safer option is to cross the road to the northern side of the Rochdale Canal, and to follow this as far as Black Pit Lock, where the town centre can be reached via Holme Street.

Hebden Bridge to Standedge

15 miles (24km)

Once across the A646 and the Rochdale Canal, the Pennine Way follows a broad track rising to the left to pass through Callis Wood to Lower Rough Head Farm. Beyond the farm it crosses fields to a path junction at a fence and stile, here turning left to rise to a broad lateral track near Swillington Farm.

Keep ahead across the track, ascending past a gritstone outcrop known as Doe Stones to a ladder stile. Turn right, over the stile, through a squeeze stile, and ascend Stoodley Pike. From Stoodley Pike, the Way runs west of south along the escarpment above Mankinholes to Withens Gate, where the Calderdale Way is met once more, and keeps on over Coldwell Hill to reach Warland Drain. The Drain is then followed to reach the northern end of Warland Reservoir, passing southwards along the reservoir and Light Hazzles Reservoir, before continuing across heather moorland to meet the A58 near the White House Inn. Turn right at the A58, passing the White House Inn, to reach Broad Head Drain, a man-made leat which should then be followed as it loops around Blackstone Edge Moor to reach the old packhorse road/"Roman" road across Blackstone Edge.

Ascend left as far as the Aiggin Stone, turning right to head for the summit of Blackstone Edge. A clear track runs south-eastwards to reach the bridge spanning the M62 motorway, beyond which the Way passes Windy Hill transmitter, and crosses the A672, afterwards rising on to Axletree Edge and Green Hole Hill. A change of direction to the east leads to White Hill and on down to the A640 Rochdale-Huddersfield trans-Pennine road.

The route now crosses the grass and heather of Oldgate Moss to reach Northern Rocher, the first section of the Millstone Edge escarpment, that circles around Castleshaw Upper Reservoir in the valley to the west. The Way continues down the Standedge Ridge and on along a clear path across rough pastures, turning left near a small quarry. Then it finally runs out by a sandy cart track to meet the A62 just north of Little Brun Clough Reservoir.

Standedge to Crowden

11¹/₄ miles (18km)

After crossing the A62 the Pennine Way moves into the Peak National Park and the final stage of the journey southwards. From Standedge Cutting the Way follows an old packhorse trail for a short distance before it branches right on to Rocher Moss and then left as it approaches Black Moss Reservoir.

The route passes between Black Moss Reservoir and Swellands Reservoir and continues eastwards around the northern edge of Black Moss to enter Blakely Clough. Shiny Brook requires a slight deviation before the Way continues to Wessenden Reservoir and Wessenden Lodge, from where the route passes above the course of Wessenden Brook to Wessenden Head Reservoir. As it approaches the A635, the route joins the Wessenden Head road and follows this to the A635.

Turn right for a short distance along the road then leave it, left, to follow a boundary ditch rising to meet Issue Clough. Turn south-west here to the summit of Black Hill. From here head south-west for Laddow Rocks. Much of what was once quagmire conditions has been improved by extensive repairs. The route crosses the top of Laddow Rocks, never far from the edge, and finally crossing it to the valley below at Oakenclough

Brook. The Way soon crosses Crowden Brook and continues as a stony track to a T-junction a short distance west of Crowden youth hostel, where most Wayfarers spend their final night on the walk.

Crowden to Edale

16 miles (25.5km)

From the path T-junction the Way continues in a south-westerly direction to meet the A628, beyond which it descends to the dam of Torside Reservoir. Once across the dam it continues to what remains of a level crossing, there turning right and in a few strides ascending to a gate. The Way now passes Reaps Farm, changing direction to climb along Clough Edge above Torside Clough and Wildboar Grain. A line of cairns shows the way to Bleaklow Head, the highest point of which lies a short way north-north-west of a collection of tors known as the Wain Stones.

The long descent to reach the Snake Pass is difficult to locate in a north-south direction, but begins by heading south from Bleaklow Head into a grough complex, finally running down to a transverse track, a Roman road/packhorse route known as Doctor's Gate, beyond which the route reaches the A57 at the summit of the Snake Pass. Across the A57 the Way across quagmiry Featherbed Moss is now paved, and leads to Mill Hill. Here the Way changes direction as it heads downwards to Ashop Head before a short ascent on to the rim of the Kinder massif. Following the edge of the escarpment quite closely, the route presses on to reach Kinder

Downfall, across which it turns on a roughly southerly direction bound for Kinder Low, Edale Rocks and the Swine's Back to reach a broad track a short distance east of Edale Cross.

Turn left (east) on reaching the track and follow it as it begins its descent into Edale. Passing down Jacob's Ladder, the Way continues into the valley to reach Youngate Bridge just before Lee Farm, and keeps ahead to reach Upper Booth. The path now heads across fields below Broadlee Bank Tor finally to emerge at journey's end opposite the Old Nag's Head in Edale, a moment that justifies considerable satisfaction.

Well done!

Essential and supplementary reading

Along the Pennine Way, J.H.B. Peel (David and Charles, 1979)

Britannia, William Camden (John Stockdale, 1806, 2nd ed.)

50 Classic Walks in the Pennines, Terry Marsh (Sigma, 1994)

Companion into Derbyshire, Ethel Carleton Williams (Methuen & Co., 2nd ed., 1950)

The Domesday Book, ed. Thomas Hinde (Guild Publishing, London, 1986)

English Country Churches, Derry Brabbs (Guild Publishing, London, 1985)

First and Last, Roland Smith (Peak National Park Authority, 1978)

Flora Britannica, Richard Mabey (Sinclair Stevenson, 1996)

Hadrian's Wall, David J. Breeze and Brian Dobson (Penguin, 3rd ed., 1987)

Highways and Byways in Northumbria, Peter Anderson Graham (Spredden Press, 1988)

The History of David Grieve, Mrs Humphry Ward (Smith, Elder & Co., London, 1892)

Lancashire and the Pennines, Frank Singleton (Batsford, 1952)

North Pennines, Alan Hall (Dalesman, 1996)

Northumberland (The King's England), Arthur Mee (Caxton Publishing, Special Edition)

On Foot in Southern Scotland, Terry Marsh (David and Charles, 1995)

Peak District: National Park Guide No. 3, Countryside Commission (HMSO, 2nd ed., 1971)

The Peak District Park, Roland Smith (Webb and Bower/Michael Joseph, 1987)

The Pennine Mountains, Terry Marsh (Hodder and Stoughton, 1989)

The Pennine Way, Tom Stephenson (HMSO, 1976)

Pennine Ways: Edale to Kirk Yetholm for the Independent Walker, John Gillham (Crowood Press, 1994).

South Pennines, John Gillham (Dalesman, 1996).

The Steel Bonnets, George MacDonald Fraser (Harvill, 1971)

The Yorkshire Dales, Marie Hartley and Joan Ingilby (J.M. Dent & Sons Ltd., 1956)

The Yorkshire Pennines of the North-West: The Open Roads of the Yorkshire Highlands, W. Riley (Herbert Jenkins, London, 1934).

Acknowledgements

My desire was to produce a guide to the Pennine Way which was up-to-date, accurate and devoid of unnecessary detail, especially in the route description, which after all relates to a route that has been tramped into the ground for over 30 years. In this endeavour I have been supported by a number of people, to whom I am inordinately thankful.

Tony Philpin and Anne Glover of the Pennine Way Co-ordination Project gave most useful advice and background information to the renovation works being carried out along the Way, as well as providing the latest information on the realignments that have been necessary. They read the manuscript for me, and offered helpful advice.

John Needham and Chris Sainty of the Pennine Way Association gave invaluable help and offers of assistance. Colleagues in the Outdoor Writers' Guild played an important part, too. Roly Smith, the chairman of the guild had the task of editing the manuscript for the publishers, John Gillham read the manuscript and offered pages of helpful notes and background information, and Martin Collins prepared the excellent maps which support the text.

Finally, my thanks to Julie, who read the manuscript before anyone else did, and raised numerous points of clarity and detail, all of which were taken on board, and for which I am immensely grateful.

Dalesman Walking Guide Series

The Dalesman Walking Guide series is edited by Terry Marsh, one of the country's leading outdoor writers. Each edition is packed with detail given by experts with years of experience of walking the area. This series is aimed at the keen walker who is either familiar with the area or exploring a new walk, and who wants a reliable pocket sized guide with detailed colour maps showing the routes and main features.

NORTH PENNINES
Alan Hall 1-85568-105-6 165mm x 100mm 224 pages £7.99
WHITE PEAK
Martin Smith 1-85568-099-8 165mm x 100mm 224 pages £7.99
CLEVELAND WAY
Martin Collins 1-85568-113-7 165mm x 100mm 128 pages £6.99
SOUTH PENNINES
John Gillham 1-85568-106-4 165mm x 100mm 224 pages £7.99
DARK PEAK
John Gillham 1-85568-100-5 165mm x 100mm 192 pages £7.99
PENNINE WAY
Terry Marsh 1-85568-108-0 165mm x 100mm 192 pages £7.99
To accompany the series:
MOUNTAIN SAFETY
Kevin Walker 1-85568-112-9 165mm x 100mm 256 pages £8.99
A bible for all those who venture outdoors, be it camping, walking or climbing, with detailed advice on subjects ranging from choice of equipment to rope-work, survival and weather conditions, map reading and river crossings. Ideal for individuals as an essential guide for their own safety or as a reference book for group leaders wishing to give instruction on mountain safety.

Dalesman also publishes a successful pub walks series as well as books of shorter walks for families. If you wish to order any of the above books or would like a catalogue showing all Dalesman publications contact: Dalesman Publishing Co Ltd, FREEPOST LA1311, CLAPHAM, Lancaster, LA2 8BR (015242 51225).